Off the Court

Off the Court

BY
ARTHUR ASHE

with Neil Amdur

NAL BOOKS
NEW AMERICAN LIBRARY
TIMES MIRROR
NEW YORK AND SCARBOROUGH, ONTARIO

NAL BOOKS TRADEMARK REG. U.S. PAT. OFF. AND
FOREIGN COUNTRIES
REGISTERED TRADEMARK—MARCA REGISTRADA
HECHO EN HARRISONBURG, VA. U.S.A.

SIGNET, SIGNET CLASSICS, MENTOR, PLUME, MERIDIAN AND
NAL BOOKS are published *in the United States* by
The New American Library, Inc.,
1633 Broadway, New York, New York 10019,
in Canada by The New American Library of Canada Limited,
81 Mack Avenue, Scarborough, Ontario M1L 1M8

Designed by Alan Steele

Library of Congress Cataloging in Publication Data

Ashe, Arthur.
Off the court.

1. Ashe, Arthur. 2. Tennis players—United States—
Biography. I. Amdur, Neil. II. Title.
GV994.A7A36   796.342′092′4 [B]   81-11027
ISBN 0-453-00400-8   AACR2

First Printing, September, 1981

1 2 3 4 5 6 7 8 9

PRINTED IN THE UNITED STATES OF AMERICA

To that nameless slave girl off the H.M.S. *Doddington,* and her daughter Lucy, her granddaughter Peggy, her great-grand-daughter Peggy, and her great-great-grandson Hammett, all of whom were born, lived, and died as slaves.

Acknowledgments

Many people have participated in the preparation of this book. The idea started with a phone call from Bill Cosby after my heart operation. Thanks are due to my literary agent, Fifi Oscard, for helping me through it all.

I owe a special debt to Frank Craighill, Donald Dell, David Falk, and Carol Gibson, my secretary, for their help over the past year. They kept the pieces of my life tied together during the writing.

Much of the credit for compilation of the assorted chapters of my life goes to Joel Dreyfuss, who spent many, many hours helping me put the whole story together. It was through him that I was able to add some coherence to the beginning.

I'm truly grateful to Susie Adams of *World Tennis Magazine* for allowing me to freely use all past issues during my research; to Steve Flink, also of *World Tennis,* for his expert compilation of my tournament record; and to Jeff Barstow and Alex McNab of *Tennis* magazine, who pored over many photographs for inclusion in the book.

Thanks also go to Nerissa Johnson, both for the photographs from her collection and for being my surrogate mother during those hot, humid summers in Lynchburg, Virginia, in the mid-50s.

My wife, Jeanne, has been more than understanding and patient during the past year, and her photographs beautifully grace these pages. The insights I gained from her reading of the manuscript have helped it, me, and us.

My editor, Joan Sanger, is due tremendous praise for her dedication, support, and guidance. Without her, the book could not have been done. My thanks also go to

Acknowledgments

Julian Hamer, Maryann Palumbo, and Alison Husting of NAL Books.

I'm also grateful to my fellow professional tennis players who unwittingly played their parts in my life. After all, the real fun and enjoyment was in the "playing" rather than the "winning." And it was fun while it lasted.

A special note of thanks to Rod Laver, who provided me with a continuing example of how the game is played. My ultimate *bête noire,* winner of two grand slams, he was *the* player of my generation. I will recount with pride my three wins over him.

And finally, thanks go to the members of my family, who have been pillars of stability and understanding for all my thirty-eight years. They have set an outstanding example for anyone to follow. I only hope I can follow in their footsteps.

Contents

No Man's Land

Jeanne grabbed my arm. My knees were shaking, and I was sweating. "You're shivering," she said, looking down with a studious, controlled calm. "Are you cold?"

"No, just scared to death," I replied, for one of the few times in our marriage not knowing what to say to my wife. Staring up at the ceiling lights in the emergency room of New York Hospital, I wondered if I would die quickly. An IV bottle over my head dripped slowly into the tube in my left arm. My right arm was wrapped in the black band of a blood-pressure machine. Seven cold spots on my chest marked the leads of the electrocardiogram machine that beeped a rhythmic confirmation of life or death.

"Are you feeling any pain?" a young resident asked, leaning over the metal table on which I was lying. A few minutes earlier, he had injected some morphine into my arm. My chest felt squeezed from all sides, as if caught in a vise, and the pressure had no outlet. The pain was excruciating.

"How strong is it?" he continued, holding up five fingers as a sign of the strongest pain gradation. I shook him off. When he put up four fingers, I felt compelled to nod.

The metal table was chilled by the room's air-conditioning unit, yet my tennis clothes were soaked. It was not the warm July weather. It was definitely fear, and I imagined how prisoners of war felt when they heard strange footsteps approaching in the night. What would happen next?

Earlier that afternoon, I had been giving a clinic at the East River Tennis Club in Long Island City with Butch Seewagen, a friend and formerly a nationally ranked player. I was one of the ten best tennis players in the world. I had won Wimbledon and U.S. Open singles titles, countless other Grand Prix tournaments, and important Davis Cup matches. I was a highly trained professional athlete who had had only a few physical limitations during my career. Now I was struggling to breathe.

The resident leaned over again. "Has the pain gone away?" he repeated. This time, I held up three fingers. Only once before had I ever felt such intense pain. During a flag-football game in my freshman year at UCLA, I sprained my ankle while running with the ball. But the pain only lasted for a short period, and the tongue-lashing I took later that day from my coach, J. D. Morgan, might have been worse. "What is wrong with you? Are you crazy? Have you lost your marbles?" J. D. shouted at the time. "I'm giving you a four-year scholarship to UCLA and you're risking it all on some silly flag-football exercise."

This exercise was much more serious. I glanced at Jeanne. What was going through her mind? Her family had talked her father back to life after he had suffered two heart attacks within a span of twenty-four hours.

"It was the day before the 1975 Super Bowl," she had recounted to me. "They doped him for seven hours with morphine, but all he could think about was watching the Super Bowl the next day. He was lying on a table right after he had the second heart attack, and we were standing away from the table. The doctors had him monitored, but it was a very scary moment for us. We could all hear the EKG machine. It was getting slower and slower and slower, and then my mother screamed. When she screamed, it shocked him so much he almost sat up. My brother, John, was standing next to him holding his hand. Tears were streaming down his face, and he just kept saying, 'Come on, Daddy, come on, Daddy.' We coaxed him, and he snapped out of it."

Jeanne's grip on my hand was reassuring. I listened for beeps from the EKG machine. Were they faster or slower?

How serious was my condition? What was happening to me? I tightened my grip on her hand.

Three weeks earlier, I had lost in the first round at Wimbledon to Chris Kachel of Australia, who is hardly a household word on the men's tour alongside the Borgs, McEnroes, and Connorses of the sport. Losing at Wimbledon is not like losing in Louisville. Wimbledon is the crown jewel of tennis, a shrine where titles and cups count more than money. In 1978, I had also lost in the first round at Wimbledon to another relatively unknown pro, Steve Docherty. As a No. 7 seed this time, being blown out for a second straight year carried an extra sting, even at the age of thirty-six.

"You need a vacation," Jeanne said afterward, trying to cheer me up. "Let's just get away from everything and everybody."

I'm not the vacation type. I don't work a nine-to-five schedule. I put things in my appointment book and organize my days around them. It's my nature to keep busy, but Jeanne thinks I try to do too much.

"This is one time you can say no to people," she stressed. I like to experience as much of life as possible. I've always felt I can sleep and rest when I'm dead; while I'm here, let's get it on and live life to the fullest. A lot of this thinking goes back to my childhood and the unmistakable impression left in black schoolchildren that there is not much they can do beyond being garbagemen or mailmen. You might be a policeman, but never a bank president, mayor, or chief of police. Every black kid I knew grew up feeling that certain jobs were off-limits and unattainable, that books and the Pledge of Allegiance said one thing, but once you left school, you had to live in a completely different set of circumstances. Some history books in the South, for example, said that the worst aspect of slavery was that Southerners did not economically use the slaves at their disposal, that slaves might have been better off doing something like manufacturing rather than picking cotton. You grow up with this mentality. I wanted to establish myself in the tennis world, and I knew I'd have to pay a price for anything that I did well. That's one of the reasons I resolved not to get married before I was thirty. I just wasn't going to do it. I wanted to make my mark first.

Jeanne brought a new dimension to my life. There are people who see our relationship as idyllic, and sometimes it is and sometimes it isn't. Partners in a marriage have to feel like they're needed. I was accustomed to doing my own thing all my life. I washed my own dishes, washed my own clothes, made my own bed. I was very independent. For a while, Jeanne would say, "What do you need me for? You have an office in Washington, you do this, you do that, your life is so highly organized, where do I fit in?" She was partly right.

I argued that I left enough time between appointments and didn't hurry. But Jeanne saw a different side. "When you came back from heel surgery," she reminded me, "you never really took any time off. Whenever we travel, you're playing tennis and I'm looking for a laundromat. I would like to be able to sit down at a dinner table and not have someone come over and sit in a chair next to us and start a conversation."

Jeanne understates her intelligence. She's ambitious, a wonderful photographer. All too frequently, though, she thinks her level of success is unfairly compared to mine. So she has had to figure out a way to break down the image she had of me, and I had to break down the wall I had built around myself. The more we talked about getting away after Wimbledon, the more I began to look forward to our trip. When I told Jeanne on the plane from London to Nice that I intended to have a good time, I leaned over and kissed her on the cheek.

4

Frank Craighill, one of my lawyers and a good friend, had suggested the Chateau St. Martin near Vence in the south of France. It was lovely, we had our own villa, got up late in the morning, had brunch, watched a bit of the Tour de France bicycle race on television, and spent the afternoons in Vence, Cannes, Nice, or Monte Carlo. Everything was less than an hour's drive from our chateau.

But a thirty-six-year-old tennis player is under constant pressure to keep both his computer ranking and his good physical condition. Experience counts on the court, but you have to work to maintain a high level. I ran twice a day in the hills of Vence and put in a good thirty miles during the week there. A large quarry was nestled in the side of a mountain in Vence a half-mile from our villa. Two well-worn footpaths led to the top, which was about six hundred feet above ground level. It was an ideal place to run. I timed myself the first day and tried to better my time on successive runs. And I did.

The view from the top of the mountain was spectacular. I could see the airport in Nice and the Mediterranean— sometimes blue, sometimes green, sometimes gray— stretching to the horizon. Not only is there a *nouvelle cuisine* in France, there is a *nouvelle architecture*. The countryside was littered with strange A-shaped apartment buildings that seemed completely out of place in the French countryside. The new buildings and ubiquitous greenhouses of the vegetable industry lent a strange technological air to an otherwise charming place. I suppose this is what they call progress, the price you pay for fresh home-grown vegetables in the middle of winter.

Underneath a large crucifix at the top of the mountain was a small boulder about three feet wide and two feet high. The faded black letters were still legible: "En Memoriam Robert Kennedy 1968." I was very touched by the gesture. Someone had taken the trouble to climb this little mountain with enough paint to print this epitaph. "Ethel would love this," I thought to myself. Twelve years earlier, Bobby had appeared at one of my street clinics in Washington, D.C., rolled up his sleeves, and helped me for an hour, playing in that feisty, rugged style of the Kennedys. The odds were that this French admirer had never met Robert Kennedy. Sitting on the boulder, I thought of the last time I had seen Bobby. He had stopped in Sacramento while campaigning in California and spent twenty minutes with Charlie Pasarell, Donald Dell, and myself. One week later, he was shot and killed at the Ambassador Hotel in Los Angeles. I remembered Bobby Kennedy as someone who would not run away or back down from a fight. So many times I watched him listen intently to somebody's problems and tribulations. When they finished he would look them in the eye and say, "What are you going to do about it?"

I did little during our holiday. Jeanne could not help but slip in a drop shot after I called my office in Washington. "Not once, but twice," she teased. "You did the same thing on our honeymoon."

I also called Roscoe Tanner in London to wish him well the day before he was to play Bjorn Borg in the Wimbledon men's singles final. We flew back to London on the day of the final. When we boarded the plane in Nice, the score was 4-all in the first set. I'm friendly with both players, but I was pulling for Roscoe. As we landed at Heathrow Airport, the captain told us that Bjorn had won in five sets. For sure, Borg was writing a permanent place in the record books.

On the way back to New York, perhaps inspired by Bjorn's mastery, I decided to make the best of the rest of the summer. I went to the Sports Training Institute on East Forty-ninth Street every day during the following week and really pushed myself. It was important to be in the best possible condition for the heat and long matches ahead.

The next stop was the Head Cup in Kitzbuhel, Austria. Kitzbuhel is tucked in the mountains two thousand feet above sea level, and the tennis balls fly a bit at that altitude. A player who is not in shape is also more likely to run out of gas quickly.

At the Munich airport, Jeanne and I bumped into Vitas Gerulaitis. Vitas and I agreed to split the cost of a Mercedes for the week, although Vitas, with his frenetic lifestyle, has been known to splurge on more than rental cars. After we arrived at Kitzbuhel, Vitas and I had a two-hour practice session while Jeanne napped. Even getting adjusted to slower clay courts, I felt good physically. I wanted to do well because AMF-Head, sponsors of the tournament, were the makers of my racquets.

My high spirits were shattered by a call at two-thirty in the morning from my stepsister Loretta in Virginia. "Daddy's suffered another heart attack," she said. "It's minor, and he's in no immediate danger, but I thought you should know about it."

I was unable to sleep after I hung up. "Are you all right?" Jeanne asked, as I got up from bed. I nodded, but my thoughts over the next few hours said otherwise.

My mother died when she was twenty-seven. The cause of death, I had read on her death certificate, was toxemic pregnancy, brought on by hypertension and cardiovascular disease. A freak accident, a chance in ten thousand, but death nevertheless. My father's second heart attack in three years brought back recollections of death at a morgue in Colorado General Hospital in Denver in 1976. I had gone to the medical center to see a friend, George Jones, the assistant personnel director. While touring the hospital, I asked if we could visit the morgue.

"Why would you want to visit a morgue?" George wondered at the time, slightly stunned by my request.

"Because I've never been to a morgue," I said.

George called to see if it was OK. "Come on down, we're

having a sale," the pathologist said. Sure enough, as we walked in, the pathologist was sitting on a table, talking on the phone and cracking jokes to someone.

Between that room and the door that led to the morgue, you had to walk through a hallway where the cabinets were stored with bodies. Past the hallway, as George and I peeked through an open door, two bodies were on display, the chest cavities completely open. It was the first time I had ever seen a dead body like that. The man was lying with his chest wide open, but with nothing inside it. "The poor guy killed himself last night because his wife left him," the pathologist told us.

After that day, my conception of death changed dramatically. In fact, whenever Jeanne and I went somewhere on a trip or to a tournament, I would tell her, "Let's visit a cemetery." One day, we were walking in a park behind a church near Berkeley Square in London. I had never seen flat gravestones. The park was built in a graveyard, and some people who were walking there probably never even realized it. There were slabs from as far back as 1690. Cemeteries intrigue me: I love to read gravestones and see who died, where he or she came from, what the last name was.

I guess my curiosity began with seeing my grandfather, Pink Ashe, in his coffin when I was five years old. Jeanne has a portrait of his gravestone with the dates on it hanging in our apartment. My mother died less than a year later. And there was the poem I learned in junior high— I'll never forget it—"Out of the night that covers me black as the pit from pole to pole, I thank whatever Gods may be for my unconquerable soul."

I'm not a morbid character, but my mother's death and my father's first two heart attacks made me feel that my brother Johnny and I somehow had gotten off easily. I had regular checkups twice a year. In 1977, I was examined thoroughly before my foot surgery. They took enough blood to overfeed Dracula, but no one mentioned abnormalities. As a professional athlete, with a finely tuned body, I would notice any physical changes even after gaining a pound or two.

Playing on clay courts can be more mental than physical, and the news of my father's heart attack unnerved me in Kitzbuhel. Even in that lovely setting, with its gingerbread houses that looked like a backdrop for *Hansel and Gretel,* I was up a set and a break but still lost to Christophe Freyss of France in the second round. If that name doesn't ring a bell, I should point out that he finished No. 140 on the player computer that year. Of course, computers don't have to learn how to slide on clay, not to mention hitting those pressureless European balls. After dinner, Jeanne and I drove to Munich, spent the night there and caught a plane back to New York the next morning.

The first day home after a trip abroad is always the same for me. I unpack, go through mail, call my father and my answering service, and look over my schedule. We came home Sunday afternoon and spent the next twenty-four hours trying to catch up. By Monday night, I was in bed at 10:30, while Jeanne was still buried in her darkroom downstairs.

An hour later, I was wrenched out of a deep sleep by a powerful pain in the center of my chest. I had never felt this sensation before and didn't know what to make of it. The pain was not localized, and the affected area seemed to be a circle fanning out about three inches from the center of my chest. The pain jolted me out of bed. While standing, I noticed that the two little fingers on both hands felt "funny," as if they had gone to sleep. I sweated a little, wanted to belch but couldn't. I bent over in pain and walked around the bedroom, clutching my chest, trying to determine what was going on.

Just as suddenly, the pain was gone. A bad case of heartburn, I told myself, and went back to bed. Fifteen minutes later, the pain was back; so was the numbness in my little fingers. I climbed out of bed, sweating, and walked around, bent over and clutching my chest.

My father had suffered his first heart attack eight years before while walking back to his truck at Battery Park in Richmond. He felt a sharp pain in his chest. "It was all I could do to get to the truck and rest," he told me later. "My left arm went numb and I took a shot of whiskey to ease the pain. I found out later that the whiskey probably bought me enough time to get some help." Alcohol, he was told, dilates the arteries.

Again my pain went away. At midnight, I was struck a third time, but I still did not want to alarm Jeanne. I finally drifted off to sleep when the pain stopped.

The next morning, I conducted a clinic with Vitas at Crotona Park in the Bronx, had lunch with a friend on the East Side, and went across the East River to my American Airlines clinic. The day was hazy and sticky, nowhere near as warm as the afternoon in 1968 when I played a Davis Cup match against India in San Juan. That day it was about 110 degrees on the court, with 100 percent humidity. I beat Premjit Lall of India in four sets but was so painfully exhausted that I didn't think I could stand up after the first set.

Butch Seewagen and I only played an eight-game pro set before the clinic. After signing autographs near a fence that separated the court from the spectators, I had stepped under a large courtside umbrella to escape the sun when a sledgehammer hit my chest. My breastbone felt like it was caving in. I sat down, out of breath, struggling for air, frightened. It was the same sensation I had experienced the night before. This time, the pain was much worse.

Without saying a word, I tried to walk off the pain in the parking lot. But I was bent over and fighting for air when Butch, who had been in the club's pro shop, spotted me through the window and rushed out.

10

"What the hell are you doing, Arthur?" he asked.

"I have this terrific pain in my chest."

"Hold on a second and I'll get a doctor," he said. "There's one who just happens to be here."

Dr. Lee Wallace was a staff physician at New York Hospital who was playing at the club that day. He asked me to describe my problem. "I have this pain in my chest. I have trouble breathing and my arms feel funny."

"Have you felt this way before?" he asked.

"Yes. Last night. Three times."

"I'm going to take you to the hospital right now to have you checked out," he said. His voice was calm, but firm.

"OK," I said. "Just let me go and get my wallet and racquet and . . ."

"Nope," he said, cutting me off. "We'll ask someone to get those things—they don't matter right now. We don't have time for that. You must go now."

I'll never forget the ride. Thank God, we just happened to be near the Fifty-ninth Street Bridge, and it wasn't busy. It was about three-thirty in the afternoon, so the rush-hour traffic from Long Island City to Manhattan had not started. Butch drove; I sat in the front, clutching my chest. Dr. Wallace was in the back. We made small talk, touching on everything except the pain.

The seriousness of my situation sank in after we arrived at the hospital. While Butch phoned Jeanne, Dr. Wallace grabbed the resident on duty and told him, "I want Mr. Ashe admitted very quickly as a heart attack patient."

I took priority over everybody else, not because I was Arthur Ashe, tennis player, but because heart attack suspects are given priority over nearly every other sort of emergency. Within ten minutes of the time we left the club, I had an oxygen mask over my face, IV needles in my arm, and an EKG machine monitoring my heart beat.

Fighting the reality of what had happened, thoughts raced through my mind—from visions of my father and Jeanne to the thought of that morgue in Denver.

11

Poor Jeanne. She had rushed from our apartment on East Seventy-second Street to New York Hospital only to have the nurses initially refuse her admittance.

"It was really frustrating," she would tell me the next morning. "I'm standing there in the hall, listening to these nurses talking in a little room where they monitor their patients. One of them says, 'Have you heard, Arthur Ashe is here, he had a heart attack?' And I'm thinking, 'What do they know? I don't believe that.' "

I spent two days in the intensive-care unit and another day-and-a-half in coronary care before the results were conclusive. An enzyme test was the final proof. I had suffered a myocardial infarction.

2

Daddy

The way Daddy told the story, he was driving Mr. William Thalhimer to the outskirts of Richmond to see a man about a piece of property. It was during the Depression, the man needed money, but it irked him that Mr. Thalhimer, a Jew, was going to buy his piece of real estate. The fact that Thalhimer's Department Store was (and still is) the Bloomingdale's of Richmond meant little to the man.

"You should have heard him," Daddy recounted to my brother Johnny and me one day. "He called Mr. Thalhimer all sorts of things. Mr. Thalhimer never said a word. When the man finished all his ranting and raving, they closed the deal."

"Where were you, Daddy?" I asked, curious about how he knew so much.

"I was leaning on the fender of the car with my arms crossed, listening and watching. Just listening and watching."

"Didn't it bother Mr. Thalhimer what the man said?" I persisted.

Daddy smiled. "On the way back to Richmond, I asked Mr. Thalhimer why he took all that guff. He said, 'I came out here to buy that land and the end result is I got the land. It's mine now. He can curse me out all he likes.' "

Daddy was a practical man. He also was a hustler. *Hustling* is a much-used term in black circles, especially in the South. It doesn't mean to swindle someone out of something; it means working two or three jobs to make ends meet. A hustler is someone who doesn't mind working hard to get what he wants out of life, someone who is practical enough to recognize that if something needs to

13

be done, he will figure out a way to do it, even if it may involve some sacrifice.

The incident with Mr. Thalhimer left a strong impression on Daddy. He got to know people. He kept his eyes and ears open. He was clairvoyant. Very seldom did situations catch him unprepared. When it got cold in the winter, we never had to worry where the heat was coming from.

"Get in the truck, Arthur Junior," he would announce with a firm voice that left no room for fooling around. He always called me "Arthur Junior."

"Where we going?" I would plead, more eager to play tennis at the Brook Field courts next to our house than run errands.

"We're going to Westwood to get some wood for the winter."

"But it's only August, Daddy."

"Don't worry about that, Arthur Junior. When something's available today, you don't wait for tomorrow."

Sure enough, construction crews were cutting down trees and clearing land to build new houses at Willow Lawn. Daddy drove to the area, backed up the truck, cut the wood with his chain saw, took the wood home, covered it, and left it. It would stay there until winter.

My father is very handy with his hands. He can make almost anything. He's a plumber, contractor, painter. He designed and built his six-room house in Gum Springs by himself—not the way Thomas Jefferson designed Monticello—but his way.

It began when the government routed Interstate 95 through the black neighborhoods of Richmond. They tore down houses left and right, much to the anger of many blacks who were uprooted; my Aunt Dorothy's house was razed. The interstate went two blocks from Baker, my elementary school. After school, Daddy would pick up Johnny and me in the truck. Then he'd say, "We're going to pick some cinder blocks."

14

Daddy

For about thirty minutes, while wrecking crews were tearing down the houses for the interstate, we would pick out whole undamaged cinder blocks. We loaded the truck and took the blocks to Gum Springs, turned around, came right back and loaded up the truck again. One day, Daddy had more than enough lumber and bricks and cinder blocks to build his house, and it didn't cost him a dime. The only thing he had to buy was cement, wiring, nails, and trimmings. When he put on an extra room to the house in 1979, he pulled out some plywood that had been in the ceiling of the shed for about twenty years. It had just been sitting up there all that time.

Several years ago, Jeanne and I were going to put new windows on our apartment.

"It's not really necessary," Daddy said, during one of his visits to New York. Instead, he weather-stripped the windows for us.

Being handy must be part of the Ashe tradition. My brother and I are good with our hands, although Johnny is a better athlete than I am and more like Daddy than I am. My grandfather was a carpenter, and I imagine there were other handy souls that my father's cousin, Thelma Doswell, traced through our family tree during her thirty years of scouring the courthouses of North Carolina and Virginia to piece our story together.

The history of my paternal family in America began in 1735 when the HMS *Doddington* docked in Portsmouth, Virginia, after a long trip from the west coast of Africa. Her cargo of 167 slaves was unloaded and the ship's holds filled with Virginia tobacco, the New World crop that had captured Europe's fancy. One of the women from the *Doddington* was sold to Robert Blackwell, a prosperous tobacco farmer.

In his book on tennis, *Levels of the Game,* John McPhee noted the painstaking work of Cousin Thelma to reconstruct our family tree. McPhee also wrote that Clark

Graebner, my Davis Cup teammate and opponent in the 1968 U.S. Open semifinals, "has no idea who his ancestors are past his grandfather." I'm sure that Clark would like to know his ancestry back 250 years, but the lack of knowledge is not that important to him. For black Americans, research into our origins is a kind of shield against a barrage of propaganda about our alleged inferiority, our supposed lack of history, our response to the challenge that we should prove ourselves before we can be treated equally.

Cousin Thelma has the results of her research painted on a large canvas in her home in Hyattsville, Maryland, and she meticulously records the births, deaths, marriages, and divorces of our large family. Despite her best efforts, however, some of this history is lost forever. For example, the name of my first American ancestor didn't count enough to the record-keepers in the eighteenth century to warrant a name. She was a "slave girl," a piece of property traded for tobacco and sold to another tobacco trader, Robert Blackwell. I have tried to imagine the terror, rage, and fear of my nameless ancestor, born free, captured and transported to a strange and brutal world. I would like to think that she tried to escape, as thousands tried, or that she joined one of the sporadic rebellions that were crushed harshly by masters who could not imagine that blacks were human beings. But along with her name, any record of rebellion or resistance has been lost.

That woman from West Africa married another slave on the Blackwell plantation and gave birth to a daughter, Lucy. If she had use of a last name, it would have been Blackwell. But since she was born, lived her life, and died on the plantation, a last name had little value. Lucy married another Blackwell slave named Moses and gave him a daughter, Peggy. This daughter produced a child, also called Peggy, who married Tony Blackwell. Their daughter, Jinney, departed from custom and the narrow boundaries of the Blackwell estate to marry a Sauk Indian known as Mike. The Sauks did not use last names, but the preacher at their wedding insisted the groom have one. Blackwell seemed as good a name as any.

In 1839, Mike and Jinney had a son named Hammett. By the time he reached adulthood, the South was in turmoil. The Civil War was about to begin, troops were moving back and forth, the old ways were no longer adhered to as rigidly. By this time, the original slaves of the Blackwell plantation and their descendants had spread throughout North Carolina and southern Virginia. Hammett met Julia Tucker, and she helped continue a line that had begun in 1735. Five generations after the nameless woman came off the *Doddington,* her descendants were freed from slavery by President Abraham Lincoln's Emancipation Proclamation and a war.

Freedom must have inspired Hammett and Julia Blackwell to follow the prophets' order to "go forth and multiply." They had twenty-three children. One was my great-grandmother Sadie. She and her husband, Willie Johnson, lived in a two-story house in Kenbridge, Virginia. They acquired several acres of land and grew corn, soybeans, and—ironically—tobacco, the crop which brought us to the New World.

The Johnsons produced their share of children. One of them was my grandmother, Amelia, who at a very young age married Everett "Pink" Ashe. One of their seven children was my father, Arthur Robert Ashe, born in 1920.

Pink Ashe was, I heard, quite a character. He was reputed to have been married a number of times, and he may have committed bigamy when he exchanged vows with Amelia. There was a rumor of another wife in Washington, D.C. When my father was twelve, Pink Ashe suddenly picked up and disappeared. He was a bricklayer as well as a carpenter; despite the grip of Jim Crow laws on skilled labor, Pink Ashe could make a living wherever he went. Some years later, when my father was working as a chauffeur, he came across Pink Ashe by accident in Lincolnton, North Carolina. He and my father talked for a long time and stayed in touch as long as Pink lived. When Pink Ashe died, they brought his body back for burial in South Hill, Virginia, the home of my grandmother.

"Everybody has a great love in their life," she told me, in speaking of the special place that Pink Ashe held in her heart. "You always save a little extra for him. He's been dead thirty years, but in my mind I haven't forgotten."

My grandfather's funeral was a very personal and emotional experience for me. I don't think I cried. I was only five and a half years old. But I remember my Aunt Lola wailing uncontrollably, "Daddy, Daddy." I sat on my mother's lap through the long, highly emotional service, and I remember peering into the coffin at my grandfather. I can still see that thick mane of gray hair and the full mustache.

There were few opportunities for a young black man in South Hill, Virginia, in the 1930s. After working in the Civilian Conservation Corps, where he learned carpentry, auto mechanics, and other labor skills, my father returned to Richmond and went to work for several well-to-do Jewish families in the area—the Thalhimers, Gregorys, Schwarzschilds, and Schillers.

While working for the Gregorys, Daddy took their dirty laundry every Monday to 95 Glenburnie Road, just down the street from the Westwood Baptist Church in a small black enclave of Richmond. One Monday, he noticed a young, slender, brown-skinned woman with long brown hair hanging her family wash on a clothesline in the next yard. He introduced himself to Mattie Cordell Cunningham, and a romance began.

Daddy had a reputation in those days as being a fun-loving sharp dresser. He was solidly built, light brown, and had what was thought to be a "good job" for a black man.

Daddy

It was no surprise that he and "Baby," as relatives called her, were married in 1938 in the living room of her mother's wood-frame house in Westwood. I was born on July 10, 1943, at St. Phillip's, Richmond's black hospital.

My early childhood was difficult. I contracted measles, mumps, whooping cough, chicken pox, diphtheria, and just about anything else a child could have. "Don't let Arthur Junior stay out in the sun too long," my grandmother would warn Daddy.

The event that changed my life more than anything came in 1947 when my father was hired as a special policeman by the city of Richmond and put in charge of a playground. We moved from my Uncle Harry Taylor's house on Brook Road to a small, five-room, one-story white-frame house at 1610 Sledd Street, in the middle of the eighteen-acre Brook Field Playground. Suddenly, a swimming pool, baseball fields, and four tennis courts were outside my door. It was wonderful.

Daddy never really played tennis. "Every once in a while, I played at a court that used to be across the street from grandma's house," he would recall. But I never saw my father play tennis, ever.

But he did set one hell of an example for me. He was thirty years old and my mother was twenty-seven when she died suddenly on that March day in 1950. I remember quite well the last time I saw her alive. It was cool and cloudy, and some birds were singing in the small oak tree outside our house. My mother was in her blue corduroy bathrobe, standing in the side door as I finished breakfast. She had had trouble with her third pregnancy. She went into the hospital three days later, there were unexpected complications after surgery, and she died. The image of her standing there burned itself into my memory. So did the sight of my father crying uncontrollably after he returned from the hospital that Saturday morning.

He woke Johnny and me, picked us out of the bunkbeds we shared, put my brother on his knee, squeezed me tightly, and told us that Mama had died.

"This is all I got left," he kept repeating. "This is all I got left." All my life, I think I've tried to prove to him that my brother and I would make up for his loss. I never saw Daddy cry that way again until that afternoon at Forest Hills, eighteen years later, after I won the first U.S. Open men's singles title. But those were tears of joy.

Her body was brought to the house before taking the last ride to the church and cemetery. Mama's coffin sat in the middle of our living room, open so the mourners could pay their last respects. She lay inside, wearing her best pink satin dress and holding a red rose in her right hand. Roses were her favorite flowers, and Daddy had planted rose bushes around our little front porch to please her. He must have cut the funeral rose that morning and put it in her hand. Daddy lifted me to kiss her on her forehead for the last time.

Whether by choice or chance, the rose became a symbol in my life. I gave Jeanne a red rose on our first date and would put one in her bathroom at various occasions as a way of showing how much I cared.

Daddy asked if I wanted to go to Mama's funeral. I don't know why he asked. Jeanne now says that it may have been his way of protecting me. Maybe he thought the funeral would be too much for me. Maybe, in that situation, he wanted to share the responsibilities with me. I don't know why, but I said no. It wasn't an emphatic or emotional response, just a matter-of-fact "no." I've tried to reach whatever feelings I had at the time, but all I can remember is a certain distance from the rush of unexpected events that turned our lives inside out.

Seeing adults emotional and distraught can be a frightening experience for a child. You feel pressured to behave like them, but because you don't understand the motives for their distress, you can only retreat emotionally, which I did. My only contact with death until then had been my grandfather's funeral. I knew that people died and that adults cried at funerals. But this tragedy within my own family was too close for me to grasp. I could not yet connect the woman in the coffin to the woman who had held me on her knee, fed me, and read to me before I went to sleep, and it would be years before I could grasp its significance.

Looking back, the events of that day are abstract and distant, as if seen through the wrong end of a telescope. I went to Mrs. Rebecca Scott's house, a hundred yards away. I watched from her yard as the funeral procession left my house and made its way through the neighborhood to Westwood Baptist Church on the western outskirts of Richmond.

Later that day, my grandmother would tell me, "Your mother is gone, Arthur Junior. She's gone to heaven."

"Where is that?" I asked. "When can I see her?"

"You will see her when you grow up and die and go to heaven," she said. "If you're a good boy, you'll see her again. Then you can stay with her forever and ever."

Her words made me feel better. They also may have subconsciously affected much of my future behavior. Jeanne believes this is the reason for my obsession with understanding death: I was told as a child that it would bring me closer to my mother.

When I think of my mother, the strongest feeling I get is regret. I can remember her reading to me and encouraging me to learn. Relatives say I read sooner than anyone they ever knew. There is a photograph of her, me, and my brother Johnny, posing with the white Santa Claus at Miller & Rhodes. But I can't remember her voice, I can't remember how she felt, smelled, or tasted. More than once, I've longed for a memory of my mother that seems just beyond my grasp.

Mama's death had a profound effect on our family. Daddy's personality changed, and the sharp clothes, playfulness, and happy-go-lucky style gave way to a more serious demeanor. "A man's responsible for his family," he would tell us. "Otherwise, a man ain't a man."

It would have been easy—and no one would have blamed him—if Daddy had asked another woman, like a sister-in-law, to take care of us. But he never did that. He did it all himself, fulfilling the promise he made to my mother when she sensed she was dying.

"I didn't bring them into this world to farm out," she told him the night before her operation. "They're your children. I brought them into the world for you, so promise me that you'll raise them yourself."

"I promise I'll do that," he replied.

As one of the few blacks on the police force, with a city job, Daddy was an important man in the black community. He still talks about the turnout for Mama's funeral cortege. "More than forty cars," he said. "Blacks and whites."

Growing up black in the South, for survival and protection your antennae were always out. My grandmother often used the phrase "good white people" to describe those who helped us. She also talked about "bad white people"; the ultimate bad white people were the Klan—the Ku Klux Klan.

At an early age I got to know many "good white people." At first, I thought it was weird that Jews didn't celebrate Christmas. But throughout my life, particularly during the early stages of my tennis career, Jewish people seemed sensitive to my needs, perhaps because they were a minority group as well. Their help prompted me later in life to read and study the historical and cultural factors that led to Jewish persecution, and there are many similarities to the sad experiences of blacks.

A little grocery store in my neighborhood was owned by a Mr. Paul, who was Jewish. A kid could go in there and say, "My mother sent me for such-and-such stuff," and he would give you the food. If a kid came in and said, "I don't got no money and my mother'll pay you when she can," Mr. Paul would let him take the food and write it down. He even gave us free candy.

Other than undertakers, service station mechanics, beauticians, and insurance salesmen, few blacks owned businesses in those days. You knew there was something different about being black, and it even came down to gradations of skin color within the black community itself. The lighter your skin, the more status you enjoyed in the black community. As blacks, we learned the same beauty standards that white people learned, and these standards still exist today. Some Jewish people, for example, decide that their noses are not what they want, so they have a nose job. It may make them look more Anglo-Saxon than Semitic; however, if you keep your last name, it may still give away your ethnic identity.

I always try to look at life in a continuum. If things are moving in the right direction, my attitude switches from "should I complain to them for not doing the right thing" to "should I complain to them for not doing the right thing fast enough?" Before 1965, the barriers had not fallen for blacks, especially in the South; it was not a question of how fast but how. I could not even envision God being black because the pictures of Christ on the back of the fans in my grandmother's church showed him as white.

The fans were always paid for by the local black funeral home. But in the picture, Christ was white, with long blond hair. I grew up with an image of a white Christ, even as I questioned this image. "The Bible says that Christ had hair like lamb's wool," I remember telling Dr. Bernard Woodson, my Sunday School teacher, who was a biology professor at Virginia State College. "I've seen plenty of sheep in my time, and the hair on this man on this fan looks nothing like the hair on a sheep."

I have always had a penchant for detail. At Baker Elementary School, where my grades were A's and B's, I will never forget that day in Mrs. Virginia Jordan's class when President Eisenhower was inaugurated in 1953. One of Eisenhower's first acts was to insert the words "under God" in the final phrase of the Pledge of Allegiance: "one nation, under God, indivisible, with liberty and justice for all." Because those two words were added, I paid attention to what we had been reciting by rote for years. Were those words really intended for us? We went to all-black schools. If we wanted a cab, we couldn't ride Yellow Cabs because they were for whites only. When I took the Number 6 bus to my grandmother's house, I had to sit behind the white line. All the people in positions of authority in the city were white. One day, I asked my father, "Is the smartest colored man (that was the term we used then) dumber than the dumbest white man?"

Daddy was slightly startled. But he recovered quickly enough to tell me, "There are smart ones and dumb ones on both sides."

There was little gray in my father's world. His rules were black or white, right or wrong, without regard to race, and there was a time when I actually feared him. Eventually, I could tell his state of mind from the tone of his voice. He was very strict, almost overprotective, and it was understandable. He had lost a father and wife in less than twelve months. He did not want to lose his children through any failure to follow orders.

"Go get my belt," he would say, if I returned late from school or forgot a chore. The belt could have been the strap in a barber shop; it was thirty-nine inches long, at least an eighth of an inch thick, and first-quality cowhide. Only grade-A leather would do for my behind. The whippings never lasted more than thirty seconds and almost always seemed to take place in the bedroom on Fridays.

There was also a standing order that Johnny and I had to let my father or Mrs. Otis Berry know where we were at

all times. Mrs. Berry was a widow in her late fifties, with
no children of her own, who lived with us for fourteen
years—the rest of her life—and helped bathe, feed, and
raise us after my mother died. Even after Daddy was remarried to Lorene Kimbrough on March 20, 1955, Mrs.
Berry stayed, and the rules remained.

The Reverend William Hewlett, the same minister who
had performed the marriage ceremony for him and my
mother back in 1938, officiated just three days before the
fifth anniversary of my mother's death. My memories of
Mama were strong, but I knew there was no alternative
when Daddy said, "I want you all to get dressed up because
we're going to Washington today. I'm getting married."
At first, I was extremely upset. I was only eleven years old.
Daddy moved back into his bedroom with Lorene, Mrs.
Berry moved into our room—her snores replaced Daddy's
—and we now had to call both women "mother." But later
I became happy for him, especially when Lorene's father,
as a wedding present, gave them five acres of land in Gum
Springs that would become Daddy's dream.

When Daddy married Lorene Kimbrough, Johnny and
I also acquired a stepbrother and stepsister. Robert and
Loretta, it turned out, were just as well mannered as we
thought we were. "Well-brought-up" was the phrase used
to describe obedient and dutiful children. We came to
know and love Robert and Loretta as if they were blood
relatives. Loretta presented Daddy and Mother with their
first grandchild, David Harris, Jr., and since they initially
lived only ten yards away from one another, Loretta and
my brother-in-law, David Sr., sometimes had trouble en-
forcing their own rules. As a grandfather, Daddy suddenly
mellowed a bit.

Daddy's sense of discipline was simple: he knew what
was best for his children and he only had to give an order
once. "There's to be no hanging around," was one of his
commandments. "If you don't have to be somewhere, you

25

should be home. A man is supposed to be at home with his family if he ain't workin' or someplace special."

Those homilies, repeated throughout my childhood, became embedded in my personality. After I moved to New York's East Side, I never hung out in the hot singles bars. It seemed a waste of time, a judgment I knew was shaped largely by values from my father. Even now, I prefer a quiet evening with Jeanne at home to needless socializing.

If Daddy was strict with us, he was just as disciplined with himself—a sensitive man with simple tastes. He seldom smoked and finally gave it up for good; he seldom drank and there was little liquor in our house except homemade wine. For a man with a sixth-grade education, who could barely read and write, he understood the game. And he made certain his children knew: he took my brother and me everywhere—on trips, to work, fishing, and hunting. After a while, we knew as much about running the playground as Daddy did.

I think the reason Daddy had us tag along on his job was to profit from his experience. We would learn how to do the things that he knew how to do because he figured we needed these things for survival. He was going on the assumption that we would grow up in a world like his. If you were black, you'd have to live in this set of circumstances, you'd have to have a certain set of tools and skills, and the more you had, the better your chance for survival. What he gave us was a message that too few black children are fortunate enough to receive: "I can set an example. I can show you how to paint, fix cars, work with tools, plan ahead. I can also show you that when I don't have anything special to do, I'm at home."

Even now, he questions how his daughter and son-in-law treat their kids. When my nephew, David Harris, Jr., was about to get his first bicycle, my brother-in-law, David Sr., wanted to put training wheels on the bike. "He doesn't need training wheels," my father said. "He'll learn to ride a bike without them." Daddy won out. David Junior never had training wheels on his bike. He might have fallen a couple of times, but my father's rationale was: he doesn't have that far to fall, the bike is short, so maybe he'll scrape his arm or something. No big deal.

Daddy instilled self-sufficiency in us. I had chores, and they had to be done by a certain time. Make the bed. Feed the dogs. Cut the wood and fill the wood box by the fireplace. Study. Some parents might say, "Well, I'll pay you something for good grades or for performing chores." Johnny and I never got paid for chores; I was expected to do them.

But Daddy sometimes surprised us. One day, I was helping him prune a big tree in front of Mr. Philip Cox's house, an all-day job. Mr. Cox was a black artist who once a week taught a bunch of us black kids how to build model airplanes. His wife was my English teacher in high school. After I finished this job, on a steamy summer day, Daddy walked over to one of the other workers and said to him, "Do you think Arthur Junior deserves to get paid?"

The other man said, "Yeah, he worked pretty hard all day." Lo and behold, Daddy gave me five dollars. I was flabbergasted.

Hard work and discipline helped shape my personality. I studied in school and read extensively because Daddy wanted me to be the "best reader in school." He borrowed money to buy a set of encyclopedias for me. I also developed a comfortable but wary relationship with money, even the pennies from Miss Claire McCarthy, a white commissioner for the department of parks and recreation. She came around every so often in her black Chevrolet and always gave me all the pennies in her pocket.

Besides working with Daddy, I had my own ways of raising money. I sold bottles and newspapers to Mr. Paul. I would save the newspapers in the basement until we had a truckload to take to The Bottom, an area at the foot of

Seventeenth Street where newspapers could be sold by the pound. Daddy let me keep a part of that money because, unlike cutting Mr. Schiller's grass, gathering the papers was something I did on my own.

I discovered the *National Geographic Magazine* in the Schillers's garage. They were throwing out a pile of magazines one day. After leafing through the *Geographics*, I persuaded Daddy to let me take them home. The *Geographic* opened up yet another new world for me beyond the boundaries of Richmond. To this day I read it and have a life membership in the National Geographic Society. It is one of my favorite magazines.

Looking back at my childhood, I see my world defined as a series of concentric circles. At the center was our house, at 1610 Sledd Street. The next circle was Brook Field, which played such an important role in defining my future. Beyond that was school, then church, and finally, the city of Richmond and the world beyond. Each of these circles was defined largely by black people because I was growing up in a rigidly segregated society. At each level, I was nurtured, loved, and challenged to develop my potential to its full capacity. The inequities imposed by racism were frustrating, but I was fortunate to be surrounded by a devoted father and other black people determined to push me along, broaden my horizons, and help me develop a sense of myself that ignored the limits white Richmond wanted to impose at the time.

The Passage

I had been standing for about twenty minutes, leaning against a tree, when I heard the dogs barking in the distance. The adrenaline began to flow, I gripped my gun a little tighter, and tried to see whether my anticipation was imaginary or real.

The weather was cold and cloudy, a typical November morning in King William County, Virginia, an hour's drive northeast from Richmond. I wore rubber boots, a rust-colored outfit with a bright orange cap, and carried a 12-gauge shotgun as if it were the ultimate test of manhood.

"Patience, Arthur Junior," Daddy had reminded me. "Don't panic. Just be patient."

The tension of waiting for a deer is similar to pursuing the seventh point of a tiebreaker. Since this was my first deer hunt, I didn't want to flub my chance. The deer hunt is one of the rites of passage for a boy in the South, like a driver's license or that first kiss. My father had fished and hunted for as long as I could remember and I had looked forward to the day when I could hunt with him for the first time.

Deer hunting is done in groups in the South because the objective is to get a deer. Daddy belonged to the all-black Brown's Sportsmen's Club, but a deer hunt was one of the few genuine bonds between black and white men in the South, an event they could share without racial turmoil and animosity. Perhaps the absence of white women was a factor.

The preparations reminded me of a council of war. Telephone calls the night before. The pre-dawn meeting. Guns. The battle dress. Although we were not familiar with old British hunting traditions, the same roles were still handed down. The master of the hunt gave everyone his place and defined roles. The master of the hounds took four or five hunting dogs to the area where the deer were thought to be. His role was to flush the deer toward hunters spread out on "stands" in a half-circle about half a mile away. Of course, as the tenderfoot teenager, I had nothing to say about the arrangements, so I was placed on the stand next to my father about two hundred yards away.

"Deer have smart ears and hawk eyes," Daddy whispered, cautioning against any noise while we waited.

After the dogs began barking, I checked everything my father had taught me about handling a gun. Hunting was different from baseball or tennis. It's not competitive with each hunter vying to see if he can be the one to bring down a deer. If the deer happens to come your way, fine. But you're not allowed to move down the road into someone else's stand.

I had developed a respect for weapons years before when Daddy's police revolver accidentally went off in the bedroom one day after I picked it up on the dresser. We left the bullet hole unpatched in the living-room wall, and it made for great conversation on two accounts: one, because it almost hit one of Daddy's fellow officers, Doc Day, who was in the house at the time, and two, because Daddy was too frightened to even whip me.

The barking grew louder in the woods, but I knew the dogs were not yet on the scent. There are two distinct barks with hunting dogs. The first reflects the ordinary excitement of being outdoors. Then there is the primeval, genetically programmed bark of the predator. This sound is nature in the raw, about as close as a man gets to the experiences of war without being in danger of being killed. It is legal, spine-tingling, and sporting.

When the sound of the dogs changed to that deeper, more urgent bark and shifted from loud to soft to loud, they were "on the trail." Once dogs lock into a scent, they simply follow their noses. They don't have to see their prey. Their heads are down, their tails are out, their ears fly.

I moved away from my tree. My right thumb rested on the bottom of the safety switch. I could read the word "SAFE" engraved just above the trigger. "When you are looking for a deer," Daddy had told me, "always look with your ears first. Don't look in the direction of the noise. Listen first, look second."

It had not rained the night before, so the ground was hard and the leaves crackled like Rice Krispies. I heard the dogs howling and I heard the deer. Branches and twigs snapped like rifle shots as the animal zigged and zagged through the underbrush. Surely he can see me now, I thought. How can he miss my orange cap?

I turned my eyes toward the sound. I would have been a good point man in the jungles of war. Quite a few point men in the military were country boys who hunted in their childhood. It also may explain how Johnny survived two tours of duty in Vietnam. He had the same apprenticeship with Daddy. Although wounded twice, Johnny made it home safely.

A light brown shape moved swiftly through the foliage in my direction. The figure moved from left to right, and I could make out a white tail, a head forward, breathing in heavy gulps. Suddenly, the buck broke into the open, exposed to me in detail by the clear dry air. His antlers stabbed in a dozen directions, his muscles quivered under his coat, and flecks of saliva outlined his mouth.

"Aim for the rib cage just slightly below and behind the front legs," Daddy had taught.

For an instant, the fear of having my shirttail cut flashed into my head. Hunters perform this operation publicly if someone misses a clear, unobstructed, "no-excuse" shot at a deer. This little ceremony is entirely in fun, but it leaves the victim the butt of jokes until he redeems himself. The

31

cutting is done after a kill, just before the hindquarters are awarded. The least damaged hindquarter goes to the hunter who bagged the deer. The other hindquarter goes to the hunter who assisted. Sometimes there are good-natured arguments about who did the wounding and who did the killing, but I've never seen the disagreements become serious.

The buck was a hundred feet away and moving swiftly across my line of vision—left to right. I raised my shotgun, lined up my sights, and slipped the safety to the "off" position.

"Aim for a lead of a foot in front of his front leg. Squeeze—don't pull—the trigger." The stillness of the woods was shattered by the roar of my double-barreled shotgun. The butt slammed into my right shoulder. The buck stopped and dropped to the ground like a sack thrown from the back of a truck. I had another load left. "If the deer falls immediately after the first shot, wait a bit on the second shot. If you miss or the deer keeps going, shoot again immediately."

I waited. It looked as if I'd bagged my first trophy with one shot. I lowered my shotgun and started walking excitedly toward the buck. Without warning, he got up and hobbled away. Before I could raise my shotgun, he was gone, leaving a flash of white tail in my mind's eye. Less than ten seconds later, I heard: "Pow, pow," the sound of Daddy's Browning semiautomatic shotgun. I could tell the hunt was over, because he was such a good shot. I raced toward his stand. The deer was lying on its side, bloodied by shots from my gun and my father's. A slight wind sent a chill through me. I was drenched with nervous sweat, but I didn't care. We would take home our share of the kill that night. I had avoided losing a shirttail. Somehow, I had passed the test.

O. H. Parrish was a very nice guy. Polite. Well-mannered. The best white tennis player in Richmond. But as I walked to the net and shook hands with him after our match in the 1961 Middle Atlantic Junior championships, I couldn't help but smile. Here too was another test—this time on a tennis court. We had grown up in the same city, held assorted sectional and national rankings, but this was the first time we had hit a ball together. And I hadn't won this match at Byrd Park or Brook Field in Richmond but in Wheeling, West Virginia. That tells you something about what it was like trying to make it as a young, gifted black tennis player in the South.

I'll never forget when Ronald Charity took Sterling Clark and me to Byrd Park to try to register for a city tournament. Ron was the first person who taught me how to play tennis. But as a black student attending predominantly black Virginia Union University, Ron knew that Byrd Park was off-limits to blacks, even for tournaments. He wanted to see if Sam Woods would bend a little and let us play.

Sam was Mr. Tennis in Richmond for a long time. But when Ron asked if we could enter, Sam said, "I'm sorry, we can't let you play."

"Why not?" Ron persisted.

Sam was too embarrassed to look at us. "The time's not right yet," he said. "I can't break the rules as they exist now." He wanted to but couldn't.

You can't compare tennis with baseball, basketball, or football. When Jackie Robinson broke the color line in 1947 with the Brooklyn Dodgers, dozens of good baseball players in the Negro leagues were waiting to follow. When Althea Gibson, the first prominent black in tennis, won national grass-court titles at Forest Hills in 1957 and 1958, there was no reservoir of black talent waiting to walk in if the door ever opened. Blacks had no identification with the sport—on or off the court. Tennis is a difficult game to learn. Very difficult. You have to be a generalist. You can't be a specialist and excel in tennis. You have to become adept in about four or five different sets of exercises, none of which are the same. Physiologically, serving a tennis ball is nothing like hitting a forehand; they're two completely different actions. Hitting a volley is not like hitting an overhead; they too are two completely different functions. You must learn how to do all of them.

I was too small for any sport but tennis. I learned to swim when I was very young, but I was always a bit afraid of water, even if there was no way to avoid Brook Pool on my doorstep. My father wouldn't let me play football because of my size, which was a disappointment, so I tried to make up for it by working harder in other activities. When I wasn't sitting on the front porch of our house buried in a book, I played baseball, basketball, and tennis.

The four tennis courts just outside our side door were used fairly regularly by a handful of black people in Richmond. The all-black Richmond Racquet Club used Brook Field as its home base. As I grew increasingly sensitive to matters of race and color, I noticed that most of the black tennis players came from the educated, well-to-do segment of our community—principals, doctors, dentists, and lawyers. As a seven-year-old trying to find his niche in a complex, segregated society, I found that significant.

The students at Virginia Union also made good use of the courts in the spring. Their campus was just beyond Brook Field and they had just two courts of their own. They practiced at the playground and played teams from other colleges. Ron Charity spent more time on the courts than anyone else. For hours and hours, he hit balls against the wall or served to an empty court. Even my untrained eye could see an unusual grace in his swing, an agility that surpassed most of his opponents.

I watched him play against another school one afternoon. He dominated his opponent and won. His name was whispered around the gaggle of girlfriends, relatives, tennis buffs, and curious bystanders who drifted over from the football fields, baseball diamonds, and basketball courts. Ron Charity, they said, was one of the best black players in the country. I was properly impressed.

The next afternoon, he was out on the courts again, working on his serve. I watched for a while. Finally, he noticed me for the first time.

"What's your name?"

"Arthur Ashe, Junior."

"Your dad runs the playground?"

"Yes, sir."

He nodded and went back to his serve. His wooden racquet flashed high above his head in the late afternoon sun and sliced through the silence. White balls rocketed to the corners of the opposing court. After a while, he stopped and looked at me again.

"You play tennis?"

I shrugged. I had batted some old tennis balls around with the twelve-dollar nylon-strung racquet that had found its way into the wooden equipment box under my bedroom window.

"You want to learn?"

I nodded. At that age, any sport was a challenge I felt I could master. "You got a racquet. Go get it," he said.

Ron Charity was a patient teacher with an understanding of my strengths and limitations. I weighed about fifty pounds. To get a tennis ball across the net and seventy-eight feet down court with a twenty-seven-inch racquet required a firm grip to withstand the torque from off-center hits.

Ron had me use an Eastern forehand grip, like shaking hands with my racquet. This is the best grip for beginners for three reasons: one, the hand is firmly behind the racquet handle at the moment the ball touches the string—a solid support system; two, it allows the best grip for an all-court attack, either down the line, cross-court, or down the middle; three, as I would learn later, it is a good starting point for future experimentation.

Arthur Ashe: OFF THE COURT

Ron stood on the other side of the net and tossed thousands of balls to me in the year that followed. I concentrated on form, my stroke, and getting the ball over the net. When I was alone and couldn't find someone to hit with me, I played against a backboard. Tennis became something I could do by myself, like reading a book, and I soon found myself absorbed in workouts without worrying about friends.

Pound for pound, I was a good little athlete—not a Lynn Swann or Kurt Thomas—but someone with agility, speed, coordination, and a will to win. If all those elements could produce timing, I was on my way. Timing is the most important element in tennis. It separates players into different levels. John McEnroe, Ilie Nastase, and Evonne Goolagong have it in spades. They were born with it. Some good players have good timing with their hands but not with their feet. John Newcombe had great hands, but his feet were average. Rod Laver's feet were A+, but his hands rated an "A." Billie Jean King had great hands and feet. I would rate my hands and feet at the "B" level.

The eyes also play a vital role in timing. People are right-eyed and left-eyed, just as they are right-handed, and left-handed, right-footed and left-footed. When someone focuses on a tennis ball, one eye—and one eye alone—does the focusing. In turning aside during a backswing, the dominant eye can lose contact with the ball momentarily. At 120 miles an hour, a tennis ball can elude the best eyes. From the beginning, I had no trouble waiting for just the right moment. Because of my lack of size and weight, however, I had to develop a semi-lob off the forehand as a form of survival.

I was aware of the limitations of my height and build and soon accepted the fact that basketball and football were not for me. But baseball was a sport that demanded agility and determination rather than bulk or height. The baseball diamond and tennis court became my homes.

36

Baseball had special meaning for all colored boys because of Jackie Robinson. Joe Louis was still a big name in boxing, but he was finishing up his career and most of us only heard about his days of glory as heavyweight champion from our parents. As soon as the Brooklyn Dodgers signed Jackie Robinson, every black man, woman, and child in America became a Dodger fan. The New York Yankees had a farm club in Richmond, the Braves, but they were not very popular with blacks because they were so slow to integrate. In 1978, George Steinbrenner, the Yankee owner, offered me a job on his staff. We talked about it over a hamburger at P. J.'s, but I had to turn it down.

One of the highlights of my summers was the baseball school run by Maxie Robinson, the father of the present ABC-TV anchorman. Even in those days, summer camps and schools were big; Mr. Robinson was the football, basketball, and track coach at Armstrong High School, highly respected and a disciplinarian like Daddy. Every day from nine to twelve-thirty, he taught baseball fundamentals. Later in the summer, the school took a trip to Washington to see the Senators play. I could have cared less if they won. I was a Dodger fan.

The trip was fun. It also was a reminder of our segregated world. Contradictions between the slogans of democracy and equality and our reality were sharpened in the District of Columbia. We could not go to certain places. Even where we were not barred, we were not welcome. I grew up aware that I was a Negro, colored, black, a coon, a pickanniny, a nigger, an ace, a spade, and other less flattering terms.

Heroes also were few—or so I thought. In the South, black heroes who made waves were discouraged. Booker T. Washington was recognized because he stressed self-help and education, and posed no threat to "the natural order of things." Paul Robeson was moderately popular among blacks. His politics, which we didn't fully understand at the time, made us uneasy. Now, he has been elevated to near deity status. Everybody admired Ralph Bunche, especially after he won the Nobel Peace Prize for his Middle East negotiations. George Washington Carver, who made the peanut fashionable long before Jimmy Carter, was highly regarded. I knew about Maggie Walker, president and founder of Consolidated Bank and Trust, Richmond's first black bank. She was the first woman bank president, black or white, in the country.

Like most black children, I held Abe Lincoln in high esteem because I had been taught that he freed the slaves, though for the wrong reasons. My one contemporary white hero was Gene Autry. I liked him because he was the underdog. Roy Rogers was the so-called "king of the cowboys," but Gene Autry was my man. My father took me to see him when I was six years old and I was impressed by the tricks he did with his horse, Champion. Playing cowboys and Indians as a kid, I insisted on being Gene Autry.

In the spring of 1954, Virginia Union hosted the Central Intercollegiate Athletic Association Tennis Tournament. The CIAA was an association of black colleges. I was ten and had been taking lessons from Ron Charity for about three years. During a break in the action, I started hitting some balls on the court that was not in use.

"Somebody wants to meet you," Ron said, approaching the court.

I followed him to a table that was under the tree outside the side door of my house. Seated at the table was the tournament director, recording scores and directing players to the proper courts. Dr. R. W. Johnson was five feet ten inches tall, dark-skinned and handsome, with wavy brown hair and a small scar on his upper lip.

"Dr. Johnson," Ron Charity said, "this is Arthur Ashe, Junior."

He shook my hand and looked me over quizzically. "I understand you're ten years old."

"Yes, sir."

"You've been playing three years."

"Yes, sir."

"You like tennis?"

"Yes, sir."

He nodded, asked a few more questions, and dismissed me. I went back to the empty court, but felt him watching me as I played. When I glanced over, he was talking to Ron. Later that day, he talked to my father for a long time.

After the matches, Daddy spoke to me about this Dr. Johnson. "Arthur Junior," he began. I could tell from the form of address that this was to be a serious conversation. "Dr. Johnson works with young tennis players. He'd like you to come down to his place for a couple of weeks in the summer so you can play against other good players every day. You'll also have a chance to travel to some other tournaments."

If the chance to play against other boys had not been enough, the word "travel" would have done it. Here was a chance to explore the world beyond the pages of my old *National Geographic*s. I had been to South Hill in the summer and had traveled to Chicago by train with my grandmother. But Dr. Johnson's offer was almost too good to be true. I had no trouble accepting.

Robert Walter Johnson was born in North Carolina, educated at Lincoln University in Pennsylvania, where he was a black All-American running back. He attended Meharry Medical College in Nashville and was a general practitioner in Lynchburg, Virginia. "Dr. J," as we called him, took up tennis to stay in shape and became a major figure in the American Tennis Association, the black equivalent of the USLTA, until his death in 1971. His obsession was the development of good black junior tennis players.

One year, while driving home from Washington, D.C.,

he saw a huge sign announcing the "USLTA Inter-Scholastic Championship." He parked his car and watched all those white boys in white tennis uniforms competing against each other. He went to the tournament director and asked if any blacks had ever played. After a long discussion the officials agreed they would accept two black finalists from an all-black qualifying event every year. The first year Dr. Johnson brought players, they lost, 6–0, 6–0, in the first round. He was terribly embarrassed but vowed he would produce a player to win that tournament. I won it in 1961.

Dr. Johnson spent most of his days at his office in the Johnson Medical Building on Fifth Street. He would come home after office hours and play tennis, frequently with some of his cronies. Miss Erdice Creecy, his lifelong secretary and private nurse, supervised his office and three-story house on Pierce Street. The basement of the house was equipped with showers, a recreation room, bar, and a shelf full of books on tennis. I read them all. Dr. Johnson had a tennis court behind his house, a rose garden, and a kennel for his hunting dogs.

Almost all our training and practicing was done in the morning and early afternoon so Dr. Johnson could have the court around five o'clock. I spent only two weeks with him that first summer but immediately ran into problems. Ron Charity had been my first teacher, and I patterned my game after him. He had worked for a long time with me on my backhand; I felt I could do anything with it. The key was a very long and early backswing. The ball had to be hit way out in front to allow for as much racquet momentum as possible. My timing on my backhand was very good. But I used a standard backhand grip, and that became the source of my troubles.

Dr. Johnson's son, Bobby, who did a lot of the teaching, wanted to change my backhand the first day I was in Lynchburg.

"Mr. Charity showed me the other way," I protested. I didn't want to change my grip. I felt I could hit all day and not miss.

"I'm your teacher now and I want to change it," Bobby said firmly. I stood my ground.

"Well, if you want Ron Charity to teach you," Bobby said, "why don't you go home?"

We had reached an impasse. Dr. Johnson called my father. Two hours later, the blue Ford screeched to a stop in the driveway. Daddy listened to the explanations of the problem. He turned to me. "Dr. Johnson is teaching you now, Arthur Junior. You do what they say." Daddy then got in his car and drove back to Richmond.

It was that simple. I always obeyed my father. They had no more trouble with me. But to tell the truth, I didn't really change the grip on my backhand that much.

During those two weeks, Dr. Johnson took me to two tournaments, the Southeastern ATA in Durham, North Carolina, and the Mall Tennis Club tournament in Washington. I was suddenly exposed to a world of black tennis whose dimensions I had not imagined. There was black tennis in virtually every major city along the East Coast and in the South, the Midwest, and California.

Because I was the youngest player at Dr. Johnson's, I had the dirtiest jobs. I cleaned his doghouse and weeded his rose gardens. Yet I had acquired these skills from my father, who often had a dozen dogs around Brook Field. I swept sidewalks, made beds, washed dishes, and rolled the tennis court. I didn't enjoy these things, but I understood this as my way of paying back, so I did those chores as quickly as I could.

I also had to use the court when nobody else wanted it, so the backboard became my challenge. Sometimes the neighbors would complain about my pounding the backboard at 7 A.M. But by the time breakfast came around, I had put in a good forty-five minutes on the board. Those

41

sessions were fantasy times. I imagined that I was Pancho Gonzales or another famous tennis player in a critical situation, at deuce, set point, match point. In practices, Bobby Johnson would make us run patterns. We had to hit so many down the line, so many cross-court, maybe a cross-court then a down-the-line, come to the net and put away the volley. We had daily contests: who could hit the most forehands without an error, the most forehand returns of serve, deep forehand shots, forehand approach shots, forehand passing shots. Then we ran through the whole series for the backhand.

I noticed early that I had more endurance than the older boys. I was smaller, couldn't hit as hard or serve as fast, but I could last longer. So I would try to go as long as I could in the practice sessions and against the backboard without missing. I also began to learn the standard tennis principles: on approach shots, go down the line, not cross-court; no drop shots from the baseline; when in doubt, hit a semi-lob deep down the middle; get 70 percent of your first serves in.

There were also maxims meant only for little black Southern boys: when in doubt, call your opponent's shot good; if you're serving the game before the change of ends, pick up the balls on your side and hand them to your opponent during the crossover. Dr. Johnson knew we were going into territory that was often hostile and he wanted our behavior to be beyond reproach. It would be years before I understood the emotional toll of repressing anger and natural frustration.

That summer of '53 was symbolic because it marked the first steps on the road from Richmond. In subsequent years, traveling with Ron Charity and others stressed the importance of camaraderie. Blacks could not eat in restaurants, so we brought our fried chicken, potato salad, and rolls in bags and passed the Thermos around the car. Spending weekends as a guest in someone's house taught me more about social graces than I could have ever learned elsewhere.

I also learned on the court. During a tournament at Barraud Park in Norfolk, I had won the first set against another boy my age and was leading in the second when I started feeling sorry for him. It happens all the time among club players, but not on the prize-money tour anymore. I decided to let my opponent win a few games by making a few intentional errors. I lost the second set, was down, 2–0, in the third, and then began to panic. I tried to come back, but the more I pressed, the more mistakes I made. I lost the third set—and the match. My opponent was elated; I was in tears, angry at myself. It was an important lesson. There would be other occasions when I felt sorry for someone, but I never again let such sympathies affect my game.

Daddy continued to stress his sense of ethics. Once I got into an argument while playing an adult at Brook Field. "I bet I can do it this way," I shouted, loud enough for Daddy to hear. He stormed out to the court.

"I don't ever want to hear you make a bet with an adult again," he warned. Daddy wasn't against wagering, just the idea of challenging someone older.

I was elected president of the student council at Baker School in the sixth grade. This opportunity to conduct meetings, approve minutes, and make motions proved as interesting as the exercise of political power. I realized I could sometimes lead people to reason. I learned the importance of language, a fact that was drummed home years later during a conversation with comedian Franklin Ajaye at the Pacific Southwest championships in Los Angeles.

Franklin and I had been talking for a while when the subject shifted to politics. I started explaining my views on black power when Franklin said, "Damn, you talk in normal conversation just like you do on TV."

43

Arthur Ashe: OFF THE COURT

I like the English language and its nuances. Morley Safer of CBS once asked Bill Buckley about his precise choice of words. Buckley replied something like, why should I not use the English language when it has so many words to express various shades of meaning? And if there is a word that expresses the shade I'm interested in, why shouldn't I use it if it's very natural and normal to me? And if people to whom I'm talking don't understand it, well, tough.

I feel the same way about the English language, particularly all the current talk of whether Black English should be taught in public schools. I have no interest in learning how to be a master of Black English. I understand it because I've heard it all my life, but I have no interest in getting a master's degree in Black English. What good is that going to do me? It's colorful, but if anybody were to publish a dictionary of Black English, it would be a very thin one. You won't progress very far if you only know Black English unless you're a poet. And I never succumbed to the notion that I should be ashamed of the way I talk because I learned to speak the English language very well. However, school teachers of inner-city black children would do well to acquaint themselves with Black English.

Street talk is sometimes considered part of the job description of being black. Whites have fallen into some of the same patterns, though. The most classic display of this came during the crisis involving the fifty-two American hostages being held in Iran. On the second night of the hostage negotiations, an obviously fatigued President Carter was waiting by the phone for the final OK from Warren Christopher in Algiers. The cameras showed Vice President Mondale half asleep, Secretary of State Muskie wearing a blue sweater and checkered shirt, and President Carter with a knit sweater. Christopher called on the phone and said, "It's all done." And then a jubilant Carter said, "Right on!" I turned to Jeanne in our apartment and said, "Can you believe that? The first thing Carter says is 'right on!' " Here was the President of the United States using the most widely accepted black idiom of the seventies. "Right on" came out of the black experience, and now everybody uses it.

But many good young black tennis players like Ronald Charity felt deprived that whites they knew they could beat were getting the rewards and the glamour. It was the same in other areas. Chuck Berry and Bo Diddley were the fathers of rock 'n' roll, but Elvis Presley made millions off it. That's an institutional pet peeve of ours. We came up with quite a few cultural fads that became national pastimes. But white parents didn't want their fourteen-year-old daughters lusting after some black rock 'n' roll star. Obviously the idol had to be white instead of black. Chuck Berry could have been packaged just as easily, yet Elvis Presley made more money than Frank Sinatra and Barbra Streisand put together.

Chuck Berry, Bo Diddley, Little Richard, the Platters, and Sam Cooke created the sound of the rural South. It wasn't until people like Fabian and Frankie Avalon carried it to Philadelphia that white America discovered it. I was never an Elvis Presley fan as a kid. I wasn't into jazz either, which also was part of the job description of being black. But I am a music lover. I felt sorry for Presley when he died, but I was moved enough to go to John Lennon's ten-minute vigil in Central Park. I wouldn't have done that for Presley. I liked John Lennon and I loved the Beatles. I have all their albums in my apartment—all of them. *Abbey Road* is a great piece of music. I wasn't even upset when the Beatles broke up because three of them—John Lennon, George Harrison and Paul McCartney—were geniuses, and I knew they could survive on their own.

When I was about eleven, Ron Charity and other members of the Richmond Racquet Club took a group of us to see our first pro match at the Richmond Arena. We sat in the one-dollar bleacher seats and soaked in the artistry of Ken Rosewall, Pancho Segura, Pancho Gonzales, and Rex Hartwig. When the match was over, I was too shy to go up to them for autographs. While the white kids crowded around the stars and bombarded them with questions and requests for autographs, I hung back. But Pancho Gonzales replaced Ron Charity as my idol that day.

My first seventeen years set the stage for the way I view the world. I grew up as an underdog, so I rent from Avis instead of Hertz now. As I played more and more against white juniors, I realized I was fighting assumptions about black inferiorities. Dr. Johnson tried to combat our insecurities by making "the white boys" the ultimate opponent.

"You're not going to beat those white boys playing like that," he would say. "Hit that to a white boy and you'll go home early," was another of his pet phrases.

Knowing that I would not be admitted to certain tournaments protected me from direct rebuffs. O. H. Parrish and some others I played against were terrific guys—period. Some others were too well-mannered to express racism crudely. No player ever refused to appear on court with me. No official ever called me a name. But the indirect rebuffs and innuendoes left their scars.

The same year that I beat O. H. in the Middle Atlantic Juniors, some kids ransacked the log cabins where we had been housed for the tournament. Officials tried to place the blame on me and phoned Dr. Johnson.

"What do you know about this?" he asked, after I had returned to Lynchburg.

"I don't know anything about it," I said, nervous that I was being implicated and that my future tennis travel could be in jeopardy. "Honest—I don't, Dr. Johnson."

"I believe you, Arthur," he said. "They said they're just investigating, but I wanted to be sure."

Not all of my encounters were harsh. During the National Interscholastics in Charlottesville in 1960, Butch Newman, Cliff Buchholz, and Charlie Pasarell asked me to join them at a movie. I turned them down because I knew I wouldn't get in—but the guys wouldn't take no for an answer. When we got to the theater, the reaction was predictable.

"You can't go in," the woman in the ticket booth said. I wasn't surprised by her statement. But I was slightly elated when Cliff said, "Well, if he can't go in, none of us will go." And all of us left.

That summer, Daddy and Dr. Johnson faced their own decision. I had won a number of important regional titles and was ranked among the top junior players in the country. Ever the realist, Daddy knew there were few opportunities for a tennis player to make a living from his sport (this was in the days before open tennis). He knew the obstacles I would face as a black tennis player; yet he felt obliged to give me, as the best young black to come along since Althea Gibson, an opportunity to go as far as I could. My peers, the juniors who had become my friends in many cases, would continue to progress, and the Californians could play all year. To keep up with them, I had to be able to play winter tennis. And there were no such opportunities in Richmond.

The solution was to spend my senior year in high school in St. Louis, Missouri, at the home of Richard Hudlin, a good friend of Dr. Johnson and another tennis buff. The move was practical because each summer I had roamed farther and farther away from home. St. Louis would be the final break with Richmond.

Everybody goes through stages in life when they wish they could change things about themselves or their circumstances. As a sophomore at Maggie Walker, I had made the varsity baseball team and pitched one inning in our first game that spring. The next morning J. Harry Williams, the principal, called me into his office.

Arthur Ashe: OFF THE COURT

"Arthur Junior," he said bluntly. "I'm kicking you off the baseball team."

I was stunned. "Why, Mr. Williams?"

"Arthur, you've got a great future ahead of you as a tennis player. You've gone further than any other black male, and I don't want to risk you getting hurt."

I was deeply disappointed. But the loss was tempered by his acknowledgment that there was something special about my tennis. Spending my senior year in St. Louis gave me the chance not only to change my tennis game but also my personality.

I was always rather shy and studious. I was good in tennis and baseball, but socially I was shy. I came out of my shell in St. Louis, partly because they made such a fuss over me and nobody knew anything about me. I could be a different person, and nobody would ever know the difference. After growing up in a community where everybody knew who I was, either because of my father or because of my tennis, I could be anything I wanted in St. Louis. Because I had a straight-A average and had already taken subjects in Richmond as a junior that were being taught only to seniors at Sumner High School, I was often allowed to study on my own.

It amazed me that I had a higher GPA than anybody else in the school. I would have been valedictorian of my senior class at Sumner, with the highest grade-point average, except that I had been in school only one year and didn't qualify. Still, grades aren't everything.

St. Louis was north of the Mason-Dixon Line, so I thought Sumner would have white students. The city had an integrated school system, but Sumner was in an all-black neighborhood. It was a different sort of neighborhood from Richmond's North Side. The kids were more street-wise, and you had to be tougher to survive. There were more kids in the school, and you didn't get that feeling of community that you did at Maggie Walker. People helped one another out in Richmond, even though there was an unwritten feeling that blacks in the public schools in the South were inferior.

Separate-but-equal was the house line for defending dual school systems in Virginia then. It was really separate and unequal. Many black teachers in the southern public schools had only bachelor's degrees. The amount of public money spent on the black schools per pupil was obviously less than the amount of money spent on the white schools per pupil. Many job opportunities were just closed to blacks, so the curriculum at black public schools was often geared toward the jobs that a black graduate could expect to find when he or she graduated, which wasn't very much. You could drive a truck, teach, become a doctor, lawyer, or undertaker; the best blue-collar job was considered that of a mailman.

Mr. Hudlin, his wife, and their son welcomed me into their home. Mr. Hudlin was a teacher at Sumner and his wife Jane was a registered nurse. Mr. Hudlin had been the captain of the tennis team at the University of Chicago in 1924 and had a tennis court in the backyard of his home. His son, Dickie, was a ninth-grader, and we got along fairly well. But I think there was an element of jealousy because of the attention my tennis got from his father. Ironically, Mr. Hudlin wanted nothing more than to have his son become a great player, but Dickie just hated tennis.

My game had evolved considerably from the deep lob that was my main weapon at age seven. Aware that junior tennis depended heavily on consistency, Dr. Johnson's plan for my development concentrated on ground strokes. This theory was a serious mistake—but fortunately, one that was correctable. Dr. J's court at home was clay and few clay-court players, especially juniors, venture to the net. He saw tennis as a game of ground strokes and sound strategy. He believed that a smart player with average strokes could out-think and beat players with better strokes and poor strategy. Up to a point, he was right, and I won more than my share of matches by out-thinking opponents.

But the appearance of California players, with their up-bringing on faster hard courts and the serve-and-volley power game, forced a change in my style. At age sixteen, I had to learn to volley in a hurry and make the jump to the eighteen-and-unders. But once I got to St. Louis, I practiced every day at the St. Louis Armory, on a wooden floor. A wooden floor is fast and slick, balls skid off the floor and accelerate after they bounce. I had to shorten my backswing to play well. With my old round-house back-swing, the ball would have been in the back fence before I started moving my racquet forward.

A fast wooden floor also gives a player a false sense of confidence about his serve. Even an average serve seems formidable when it skids off a slick floor. It could have lulled me into accepting the shortcomings on my serve, but Mr. Hudlin and Larry Miller, a white pro, told me to lean forward and put more muscle into my service motion.

I started to return serve differently. Usually, I would stand just behind the baseline and wait for the ball. Now I dropped back a yard and a half or so and charged the ball when my opponent served. I had never been comfortable charging the ball because of my clay-court background, but with my new aggressiveness, I developed new tech-niques to catch the ball on the rise. In the course of some weight-shifting drills suggested by Larry, I developed a topspin backhand, which worked very well for moving the ball cross-court as I charged forward.

I also changed my grip from the Eastern to the Conti-nental. It is a less secure way of holding the racquet for the forehand, but it allows you to hit everything—fore-hand, backhand, volley or serve—with the same grip. The disadvantage is that flat forehands are very difficult to hit with this grip. I began to observe my opponents' grips to figure out what they could and could not do.

The Passage

In November 1960 I won my first USLTA national title, the National Junior Indoors. At Christmas, on the way back to St. Louis from the Orange Bowl Juniors in Miami Beach, I stopped off in Richmond to visit my family. While I was at home, I got a telephone call one afternoon.

"Arthur, this is J. D. Morgan," the voice on the telephone said. There was a pause. "I'm the tennis coach at UCLA. We're preparing to offer you a scholarship to come out and play for us."

You could have knocked me over with a feather. I was thrilled beyond belief. I said yes even before he finished his offer. I had no idea that UCLA had any interest in me. I would get offers from Michigan, Michigan State, Arizona, and Hampton Institute later, but every junior player knew that UCLA and USC were the schools for tennis.

My father understood my elation but did not understand the significance of UCLA. He supported my decision to go to California, although he was clearly upset at having me move still farther away from the family.

Mr. Hudlin also realized the importance of my UCLA scholarship, and Dr. Johnson was as thrilled as I was. My senior year capped my long career as a junior player. After fulfilling Dr. Johnson's dream of producing a winner in the Interscholastics, I reached the semifinals of the National Jaycees and the National Juniors. By graduation, I was the fifth-ranked junior in the country and a member of the Junior Davis Cup team that traveled together that summer.

Of course, there was a great deal of fuss about being the "first black" Junior Davis Cup player, the "first black" to get a tennis scholarship to UCLA, the "first black" to win at Charlottesville, etc. Those comments always put me under pressure to justify my accomplishments on racial grounds, as if sports were the cutting edge of our nation's move toward improved race relations. The fact that this kind of accomplishment by a black player got so much attention was an indication that we still had so far to go.

51

Arthur Ashe: OFF THE COURT

The questions asked in 1960 and 1961 served to remind me of my isolated status in tennis. I played in clubs where the only blacks were waiters, gardeners, and busboys. I knew there was apprehension in some circles about my presence, but I was not about to embarrass myself or anybody else. I was polite, fairly well educated, and I knew which fork to use because I had done some catering with my father.

I was moved into the world of tennis that had little in common with the black experience. The game had a history and tradition I was expected to assimilate, but much of that history and many of those traditions were hostile to me. When I decided to leave Richmond, I left all that Richmond stood for at the time—its segregation, its convervatism, its parochial thinking, its slow progress toward equality, its lack of opportunity for talented black people. I had no intention then of coming back. And I really never would, except to see my family, and for a few tournaments and a Davis Cup match years later.

When I got national recognition as a tennis player in my senior year in high school, it was an important step in my personal campaign to overcome assumptions of inequality. But I also knew that no one in Richmond's white tennis establishment had done anything to help me to get where I was. My memories and experiences about Richmond remain firmly rooted in the 1960s. The support I got—from teachers, relatives, and people like Ron Charity and Dr. Johnson—prepared me for the life I would lead outside the South.

4

J. D.

The deep serious tone told me there was a problem. If J. D. Morgan had not been such a great administrator, he would have made a marvelous disc jockey. When J. D. Morgan talked, people listened.

"Arthur, there's a weekend tournament at the Balboa Bay Club," he began, seated at a chair in his office in the administration building at UCLA. Although J. D. was the tennis coach, he was also associate business manager of the school and later became athletic director. "Well, it's held every year," he continued, "and they usually send out invitations to the college teams. For some reason, they have decided not to invite you. So I've called you in to decide what you want to do about it."

For a moment, I was too stunned to say anything. California was the land of milk and honey, free spirits and golden opportunity. I could still recall stepping off the plane at Los Angeles International Airport a few weeks earlier, after a fourteen-hour flight. It was one of those bright, sunny California days when the sky was a deep blue and the September air was so crisp it seemed to snap. But if I thought my break with the past was complete, J. D.'s words jarred me back. There would be no more riding in the back of the Number 6 bus, but the sense of space, palm trees, and ethnic diversity in Los Angeles could not hide other realities.

"I really don't know if I want to make a big thing of it just yet," I said. Even seated, J. D. was an imposing figure: five eleven, large around the middle (but not fat), huge hands, and a big rear which earned him the nickname "Anvil Butt" from Allen Fox, a varsity tennis athlete three years older than I.

"We don't have to send the team, Arthur," he stressed. "We can make an issue if you like. It's up to you."

J. D. had opened the door. If I wanted to protest being excluded from a tennis event because I was black, I had my chance. "I'm not sure," I said, still uncomfortable with what he had told me and my opportunity of the moment. "I've only been in school a couple of weeks and I'm hardly in a position to start fighting the establishment. If the other players don't want me to play, I won't play. There are a lot of other tournaments I can play in."

J. D. nodded. "The other players have nothing to do with it, but I think you have a point," he said, his resonant voice lingering on syllables for emphasis as only he could. "You can't make a little issue. If you want to fight something like that, you have to fight it to win it. And you have to prepare for it, get your ducks in order so to speak. There will always be clubs like that and people like that. If you want to make a career out of fighting them, your tennis is going to suffer. When you're more established, you can be a good tennis player and be in the position of fighting them on your terms."

From the first day I met J. D. Morgan, my antenna told me to trust him. After my arrival at school, he gave me the most complete rundown of a situation I ever received until General Creighton Abrams briefed the Davis Cup team in Vietnam seven years later. I didn't have to go to freshman orientation: J. D. knew everything and everybody.

"Are you prepared to study five hours a day?" he asked, after I told him I had thoughts of majoring in engineering or architecture.

"Five hours a day?"

"Yes, Arthur. Engineering and architecture are very difficult disciplines. I don't doubt you can do the work, but unless you have your heart set on a career in those fields, I suggest you try business administration."

I couldn't answer J. D.'s five-hours-a-day question at the

Arthur Ashe, Jr., age twelve.

"Bobby" Johnson, Jr. (left) and Dr. J.

A few of Dr. J.'s charges. Left to right: Charles Brown, Arthur Ashe, Ethel Reid, Hubert Eaton, Joe Williams.

Listening to instruction from UCLA coach J. D. Morgan.

Ashe with Bobby Kennedy, Charlie Pasarell, and
Donald Dell in Washington in 1966.

A "bemedaled" Lt. Arthur Ashe, Jr.

The "mod" 1968 Davis Cup Team. Left to right: Donald Dell, Dennis Ralston, Stan Smith, Arthur Ashe, Charles Pasarell, Clark Graebner, Bob Lutz. (Bob Peterson, LIFE Magazine, © 1968 Time, Inc.)

Ashe's first U.S. Open win in 1968, over Tom Okker (left). (Russ Adams)

A private "public" moment with Arthur Ashe, Sr., following the 1968 U.S. Open win. (Tony Triolo/*Sports Illustrated*)

The third Davis Cup win over West Germany in 1970. Left to right:
Jurgen Fassbender, Wilhelm Bungert, Ed Turville,
Stan Smith, Cliff Richey. (Russ Adams)

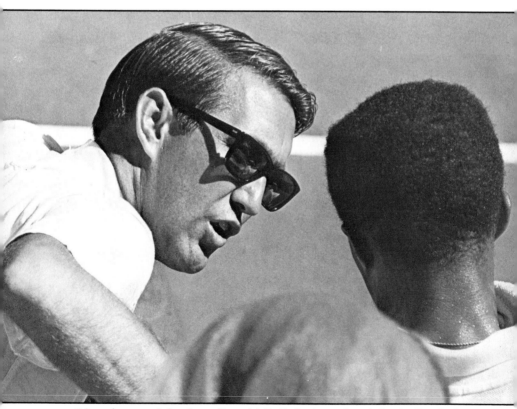

Listening to advice from Donald Dell during a break in the Davis Cup
tie match against Manuel Santana of Spain. (Russ Adams)

A tennis clinic in Uganda, 1970. (John Reader/*Sports Illustrated*)

The pro-celebrity event at Caesar's Palace in Las Vegas, 1973.
Left to right: Alan King, Johnny Carson, Ashe.

One of Ashe's Philip Morris visits to NATO headquarters with General Alexander Haig (center) and Duke Ludwig, Philip Morris, Europe. (SHAPE Photo)

A win over a young Bjorn Borg at Forest Hills Open, 1973. (Russ Adams)

time, but I knew I had to think seriously about my future beyond tennis. After some reflection, business seemed more logical; J. D. had other advice on that first day.

"Arthur, you're a big boy now," he warned. "You're going to be here for four years. All my boys graduate. I'll know who your teachers are, and in some cases, I'll know if you're having trouble before you do. You're here on great recommendations. I know you'll do well. The most important thing for you to begin today is to learn to organize your time. It's difficult enough for freshmen who don't play varsity sports. It'll be tougher for you. Don't waste your time, plan ahead, and do your papers early. This is a tough school academically. Don't get behind."

J. D. handed me a slip of paper with his home telephone numbers. "If you think you've got a problem that you can't solve, give me a call any time," he said. "Don't worry about waking me. I only sleep six hours a night anyway."

I phoned J. D. after I flunked my freshman essay and was put in a remedial English course. All incoming freshmen had to write an essay, which was graded to determine their course level for that semester. Writing had always been one of my favorite subjects, from the time I wrote a letter to the editor of the *Richmond News-Leader* to protest plans to close the Brook Field Pool. I was quite proud when the paper published my letter.

I was equally as proud the day that my high school English teacher, Mrs. Cox, the wife of Philip Cox, the artist, picked out one of my essays to read in class. She had asked us to put down the most important thing we had learned in her class that year. Most of my classmates put down answers relating to English. I wrote that I had learned not to accept everything at face value just because you heard it from a teacher, that we had to scrutinize, criticize constructively, and question everything because black people were too much like sheep. Once they accepted a certain person in a certain position of authority, I wrote, they would believe everything that person said and could be led down the wrong road. Mrs. Cox didn't identify the essay as mine, but I could tell how pleased she was.

The shock of flunking the freshman essay wore off, I got a B in the course, and was moved into regular English the second semester. But there were other culture shocks for me at UCLA, like the Balboa Bay Club incident and the clash of motivations and class backgrounds between black male students and black female students. You could tell the difference between the black males and females by the way they dressed, and it wasn't a simple matter of skirts versus pants. The black women, who came from upper-middle-class backgrounds, could afford it.

I've always been in favor of the Catholic rule of wearing uniforms to school. In Richmond, people knew if you were poor because it showed in the way you dressed: your clothes were raggedy, the soles of your shoes were coming apart from the top. Kids were teased because they had a hole in the seat of their pants or put cardboard in their shoes. The ones taking the jokes didn't think it was funny. If your father was a doctor, you dressed well, and it also showed. Since jeans were considered play clothes, not to be worn to school, you felt self-conscious if you wore them.

At UCLA, I thought black women always dressed chic because they were looking for husbands. For a long time, I assumed they were stuck up and only associated with the ones in my dorm. In fact, one of the first girls I met at Sproul Hall, the coed dorm where I spent my first two years, was Susan Ikei.

Susan was a Nisei, born in California of Japanese parents. Her father was a cook who had been in the internment camps during World War II. She had never dated a black before. She was just as intrigued with me as I was with her. We took classes together, studied together, went to football games and school dances together; we were crazy about each other.

J. D.

We spent hours talking about prejudice. Both our fathers had working-class backgrounds, but her parents still had the old Japanese customs although they lived in Van Nuys. She had a quick, high-pitched laugh, and I could often sense the struggle between Susan, Nisei, and Susan, the college freshman. She was very bright, deferred to me a bit (although she spoke her mind), and did not like Oriental men. That bothered her a great deal.

"I just don't find them attractive," she explained. "But you, you're different. And I was actually afraid to date Negro boys in high school." I met her parents one day at their home and they were very nice to me. Very polite. You could tell they were pleased to have a daughter at UCLA.

She and I talked about the incident with the Balboa Bay Club. The Japanese were also excluded from many of the private clubs. She thought I shouldn't make a big thing of it. I felt good that Charlie Pasarell, who had enrolled as a freshman with me, decided not to play.

Charlie came from a wealthy family in Puerto Rico. We had gotten to know each other well at junior tournaments and Junior Davis Cup trips, and going to UCLA expanded our friendship.

"I never hear about the Japanese starting racial trouble anywhere in the U.S.," I said. "Why is that?"

"Because we are secure in our heritage," she said. "Ours is a nation with a long, proud and glorious past. Even though my father spent time in those World War II camps, he is not angry about it. In fact, he wanted to go because he felt safer and it was a time of learning our language again. He hardly spoke English while in the camps. His big fear was 'what if the Japanese win the war?' "

I was fascinated by the foreign students. If the trip from Richmond's Broad Street to Hollywood's Sunset Strip seemed like a quantum leap, the shock for foreign students was even greater. My adjustment had to do with attitudes, but theirs had to do with the abundance of things Americans took for granted: food, cars, houses, clothes, and money.

My conversations with foreign students lasted for hours. Sometimes the Africans would talk loosely with the black American athletes. Accustomed to direct, unequivocal colonialism, they asked probing questions about our situation. "Aren't you so-called student athletes exploited and underpaid?" By their reckoning, if five guys in uniform could fill the Sports Arena and all they got was tuition, books, and room and board, something was wrong.

"How can you Negroes call yourselves Afro-Americans? You've never seen Mother Africa. You don't speak any African languages. You don't know our customs. None of you ever visit the Afro-Asian Cultural Center here. All I see you do is play cards and play pool when you're not in class."

They were right about some things and wrong about others, but the excitement for me was my first encounters with real Africans. To see their authentic clothes and their scarification marks and to discuss issues with them was pure intellectual and emotional pleasure.

We also had tough questions of our own. "You don't have freedom of speech in Ghana and The Congo, do you?" I asked one day. "Why are there only thirty-six universities in all black Africa?" and "Why didn't you write your history down on paper?" This last question was the most provocative and opened tremendous discussions about oral versus written history, origins and legacies, and the similarities between black people the world over.

One of my roommates, Jean Baker, was a student from Haiti. He was wealthy, educated in Paris, suave, and a member of the tennis team. He was left-handed, and a pretty good player. But he never worked very hard at his game because tennis was just a hobby for him. He had problems with some of the black athletes because he was a light-skinned, straight-haired mulatto. There was an automatic assumption that light-skinned Caribbean people had aristocratic airs and thumbed their noses at other blacks. Jean was not like that. But since he wasn't white and looked foreign, he was teased a great deal by the other athletes for not being "black enough," an issue I was soon to face. More misconceptions.

As a black in a sport dominated by whites, I was a convenient target. Yet there was very little I could do in those days because most tournaments were held in exclusive places like the Los Angeles Tennis Club, Beverly Hills Tennis Club, or the Racquet Club in Palm Springs. In my own way, I tried to express my feelings; for example, I never accepted future invitations to play at the Balboa Bay Club, even when they decided I was good enough to be accepted. But for many blacks, my position was not defined enough.

"If you're going to maintain your identity and your equilibrium," Tebbie Fowler tried to tell me one day, "you can't associate too much, you can't assimilate. You can commingle, but not assimilate."

Tebbie was a black baseball player on scholarship. As a sociology major who grew up in Compton, a predominantly black community in Southern California, he had a slant. Years later, I got into an argument back home with a former classmate, Ernest Walker, who thought I didn't identify enough with the black community.

"What are you doing for black kids?" Ernest said, challenging me one night at a party that a friend of my father's, Mr. Wesley Carter, had thrown for me. I heard that question continually from reporters from the time I became a ranking player at UCLA, particularly when the black cultural revolution began to assert itself. When confronted by black members of the media I would usually come back with, "Well, how many black kids in the mid-sixties have you taught how to handle a microphone?" I said that because I wanted them to know that just because you're a personality doesn't mean that you're the only one with a responsibility for passing down knowledge. But there was nothing I could tell Ernest or some of the other black students at UCLA that would satisfy them. You can do clinics—and I've done my share—but you can never do enough. They want you to be great as well as spend all your free time in the black community, and you can't do both. You can't be No. 1 on a tennis court and spend all your time in the black community. Muhammad Ali didn't do it, Martin Luther King didn't do it, no one's done it. It can't be done. If I had the luxury of being able to devote all my time to tennis, instead of being diverted every once in a while into black causes for whatever reasons, I would have been a better player. There's no question in my mind. There is little Swedish or Nordic peer pressure for Bjorn Borg to get involved with the plight of oppressed Swedes.

In some respects, however, Tebbie Fowler was right. At some point, you have to face up to your place in American society. To find out what that place is, you have to determine how far you can walk out on the plank without feeling uncomfortable by yourself. Some people can only do it en masse; some people, like Ali and Dr. King, didn't mind going out there by themselves. Tebbie dated some of the white girls at UCLA. "I go out with them," he told me, "I may even sleep with a few, but I'd never marry one."

I was disillusioned into generalizing about whites possibly because of the whites I knew and associated with at UCLA—Dave Reed, Dave Sanderlin, Charlie Pasarell, J. D. Morgan. Pasarell is still a very close friend. But I had to know where I was going and how far I could go. So instead of joining, say, Zeta Beta Tau, a white fraternity on campus, I joined Kappa Alpha Psi, a black fraternity. I couldn't join some white fraternities at UCLA anyway.

J. D.

It would have been difficult for me to avoid getting involved in politics. Growing up in the South in the 1950s, studying at UCLA in the 1960s, even playing tennis planted seeds of confrontation.

My first contact with politics began at home. My father ruled like an autocrat: he determined the "common good"; he broke all ties and made all the rules. He had an absolute veto. The first authority figure I recognized outside our home was the principal at Baker Elementary. She was the boss; the teachers were her staff. Although I served as a student council president in the sixth grade, I did not understand the importance of the Brown decision, and its impact on segregation and equality. Our teachers made a big deal of it, but the only thing we understood was that we might have some white classmates.

At UCLA, I was geographically removed from most of the major activities of the civil rights movement. The marches and sit-ins and arrests were on the front pages every day, but I was a long way from them. South Africa was still an issue for the future. However, I was not isolated from President Kennedy's assassination in 1963; I can still remember walking from the dorm to an economics class and spotting students massed in front of the student union whispering and listening to transistor radios. The student union is a political gathering spot on all college campuses. It's also where I met Ron Karenga. Karenga was a short, bald-headed graduate student, who headed a group called US, which meant "us slaves." He wore great big dark glasses, a Fu Manchu mustache, bright dashikis, and was known as the heaviest, baddest black dude on campus.

He could usually be found outside the student union discussing his philosophy of self-defense for the black community. On this particular day, I listened to him rapping for about thirty minutes until it was just the two of us. We talked about the black struggle, California-style.

Arthur Ashe: OFF THE COURT

Karenga had formulated the concept of "Kwanza," the East African harvest festival, as a substitute for Christmas, which he saw as a white, Christian commercial ripoff. He also popularized the Seven Principles of Swahili that are used by Julius Nyerere of Tanzania. If black people didn't start learning and enjoying their culture, Karenga argued, they would become "white Europeans."

I had never heard this doctrine before. And with my southern background, I wasn't sure he understood where I had come from and what I was up against.

"It's attitudes like yours I'm trying to change," he said. "Look, you're the cream of the black crop, you're in college, you're going to do fairly well in life. If I can't convince you, then what do you think about the black masses?"

I couldn't say that his argument was wrong. It depended on whether or not it suited me, at the expense of everything else. I never talked to Karenga again, but I followed his struggle in the future with the police and the Black Panthers. And what we talked about that day was important for me.

Being shut out of Balboa Bay hardened some of my attitudes toward private clubs. If you look in the back of the USTA *Guide,* you'll find hundreds of member clubs. A lot of these clubs have discriminatory memberships and nobody has challenged them. The Kentucky State Juniors was one of the five big junior tournaments when I was coming up. I wasn't allowed to play the Kentucky State Juniors because they were played at the Louisville Boat Club, and the club would not allow blacks. I couldn't play the Virginia State Jaycees because the tournament wouldn't accept my entry. Thus, I could not qualify for the National Jaycees for four years.

Country clubs or private clubs should be allowed to choose their own members as they see fit. But if club rules invade the public domain, the rules should be changed. In

62

the case of the West Side Tennis Club, which hosted the National championships and U.S. Open before it was moved to Flushing Meadow, their discriminatory policy was hypocritical and wrong. However, it has changed now.

My feelings on private clubs are not bitter, because many clubs treated me kindly. When I played a tournament at the Racquet Club in Palm Springs three weeks after the Balboa Bay episode, Charlie Farrell, the television personality and Julie Copeland, the club hostess, introduced themselves and said, "We've followed your tennis, Arthur, and you're always welcome."

I was quite flattered that Dinah Shore and Barbara Marx, who was later to marry Frank Sinatra, would even talk to me at the time. Even Pancho Segura, then the pro at the Beverly Hills Tennis Club, let me give playing lessons to some of his members. Segura charged fifteen dollars an hour; I kept ten and gave him five. Charlie Pasarell and I often wound up playing mixed doubles with Dinah and Barbara.

"If you fellas ever want to use the court at my house, you're always welcome," Dinah told us. We never took her up on the invitation, but it was genuine.

Dinah and I never talked about race or politics. She was a good player, with a decent forehand. She enjoyed tennis and didn't care about the outcome. I've heard it said that you can tell someone's personality by the way they play tennis. In the case of Ethel Kennedy, who's very tenacious with a gritty forehand, that's certainly the case. Sidney Poitier is as silky on the court as he is on the screen, and Rod Steiger has a brutish first serve that goes with the type of characters he plays.

Allan Fox, a former top-ranking player who attended UCLA, once said that I didn't want to grind out points, that my game was more "quick-kill." I guess his assessment fits my philosophy that life means taking risks. Playing it safe can be boring. Even if you take a risk and it doesn't pan out—what the hell, you can try it next time. I always knew what the down side was. In tennis, the down-side risk is losing the point. But maybe you'll win the next point, or play it a little more safely. People have always thought of me as studious, and that's true. I've always gone out on the court with an idea in mind, a technique I learned from Dr. Johnson and then again from J. D. Morgan. There's a good chance that I might have gone farther if I had put a bit more planning into what I was doing. The day before I was to play a Davis Cup match against the West Indies in Kingston, Jamaica, our coach, Pancho Gonzales, asked me, "All right, what are you going to do tomorrow?"

"I'm just going to play my game," I said.

"What are you talking about?" Gonzales responded, staring at me as if I were mad. "That's a bad attitude to have. Your game should be whatever it takes to win."

From the time I first saw Gonzales during one of his one-night stopovers in Richmond, he fascinated me—perhaps because of his powerful game and Mexican-American background. I got to hit a few balls with him when I played the Eastern Juniors at sixteen. The pros were in town and he was practicing on the grass at the West Side Tennis Club one day when the tournament director said, "Pancho Gonzales has agreed to hit a few balls with you kids, so get in line." We all ran to get in line, and I hit about three or four balls with Gonzales. He didn't remember it, and it wasn't until I arrived at UCLA that I could soak up his knowledge.

He practiced at the Beverly Hills Tennis Club and was always giving pointers to the kids, especially those he liked. I don't know if it was because I was black or polite, but he took a liking to me and helped me refine my serve.

"Toss the ball more to the right—into the court," he would stress. "Lean into the shot. You serve with your body, not with your arm. If you serve with your arm, you'll get tired." I never saw Gonzales play when he was twenty or twenty-one. But I played against him when he was thirty-seven and still battling Rod Laver, so I have a fairly good feel of his game. He, Laver, and Bjorn Borg would have to rank as the best of all time.

Gonzales was a fierce competitor, but he would have been very vulnerable on his forehand side with Borg. There wasn't much he could do with his forehand, though it was very steady. His backhand was basically a chip. It could have been a hard chip side spin, for passing shots, but it really didn't have the sting of a Connors backhand or even Borg's backhand passes. Gonzales's backhand reminded me of Vitas Gerulaitis's, and Vitas can only hit that flat punch. He can't do anything else with it except lob—which he does well—unless he gets into position.

Laver would have been very vulnerable at the net against Borg. Laver never had a great volley. He had very quick feet, but his hands weren't that sure. He flubbed a lot of volleys and I think Borg would have really rattled him. There is no question that Laver would have come to the net a lot. He had a great backhand floating chip approach shot, but Borg would have eaten that shot alive— he would just chew it up. I haven't seen anybody around with passing shots as crisp, sharp and penetrating as Borg's, and it's because he can hit with topspin. You can't really be sharp with underspin because it tends to make the ball float and rise. You can't rap the ball with any authority using underspin.

Borg has no stroke production weaknesses and I think he's the best that's ever played. Obviously, I'm not the most qualified to judge, because there are people who saw Bill Tilden in the 1920s, Don Budge in the 1930s, and Jack Kramer in the 1940s. But Borg has great passing shots and is very, very fast on his feet, a tick faster than Laver. He's improved his serve a hell of a lot, and I actually think Borg is still getting better. In the next five years, we'll see Borg volley more; as he gets older, he'll want to shorten points a little bit and not rely on just running down his opponents. This will round out his game. He already has the best ground strokes in the game, and the best forehand for sure. His backhand is good; very good, very steady. He gets great passing shots off his backhand. If he had played Borg, Gonzales would have been in every match simply because of his overpowering serve. He knew and understood the serve with the same thoroughness that J. D. brought into coaching.

J. D.'s great asset was his ability to motivate his players better than any other college coach. The entire student body was reduced to one man during our practices. J. D. represented everything about UCLA—good and bad— and it remained that way until his death in 1980. He never passed the buck. On his desk was a sign that read "Winning solves all problems." Not quite Lombardian, but you knew he was intensely competitive. I admired and imitated the way he sought responsibility. He was quick to take blame and credit and had a way of keeping you off-balance. You were never quite sure of J. D.'s opinion of your performance until he gave you a final critique. He might chew you out even if you won your match.

J. D.'s personalization of everything was bad in the sense that players came to rely on him a little too much. After all, a coach has to instill confidence that comes from an inner strength. If a player could only perform on J. D.'s instructions, that player wouldn't learn to think for himself. Still, J. D. left little to chance. He was the best-organized person I ever knew and prepared for every contingency. A pad and pencil were attached to the dashboard of his Chevrolet. When I asked why, he explained, "Arthur, you never know when some idea, some thought, some brainstorm will come along. Rather than take a chance and forget it, I write it down. That does two things. One, it's written, I won't lose it. Two, if I write it down, I don't have to worry about forgetting it."

J. D.

Just as he had his own way of getting a point across, J. D. conducted practice in his own way. He never allowed practice challenge matches to determine who would play what position on the team. "I'm the coach," he would say. "I choose the team and make the lineup. If we're going to win, and that's part of the reason you're here, then what matters is not whether you can beat one another but whether you can beat your counterpart at USC."

USC was an obsession for every UCLA coach, and J. D. was no exception. Our archrival was only twenty-five minutes away and our entire year depended on how we did against "SC."

College tennis was big-time in those days, before the open era. USC's team included Rafael Osuna, Dennis Ralston, Tom Edlefsen, Ramsey Earnhardt, and Bill Bond. Bond played No. 5 singles, and he was ranked tenth nationally in singles. Osuna and Ralston were former Wimbledon doubles champions.

Nobody was dying to leave college to play pro tennis. In 1963 the traditionalists in the United States Lawn Tennis Association (in those days the "lawn" was still used) rejected President Ed Turville's plea for an experimental open, and it would be five years before amateurs and pros were united.

The money on the pro circuit has changed the market now, but I would still strongly urge someone on scholarship to take advantage of the scholarship and graduate from college. Unless the player finds himself in the top fifty on the player computer after a summer of tournaments, my recommendation is stay in school and graduate. Jimmy Connors played one year at UCLA, won an NCAA singles title, and turned pro. John McEnroe did the same thing at Stanford. They're exceptions. Billy Martin should not have turned pro when he did, and I told him that. Billy was a junior whiz kid who won every junior title, but he was not ready at the senior level.

I'm a pretty good judge of talent, and I'm seldom

wrong. I wasn't wrong with McEnroe. When I watched him at Wimbledon for the first time, the year he reached the semifinals as a qualifier, I said, "This kid has it all. He's going to be great, and it won't take long." I even underestimated Vitas Gerulaitis a little bit. Vitas went a couple of notches higher than I thought he would go because he had two weaknesses—his second serve and a stiff but steady backhand. But he was fast, a great competitor who never gave up, and he had a good topspin forehand and an outstanding volley. Vitas was top-ten material, but he wound up in the top five. I told Nick Bollettieri that Jimmy Arias should not have turned pro so soon. At sixteen Arias won a round at the 1980 U.S. Open before losing to Roscoe Tanner. He needs more peer pressure to help him along.

My college career was a roller coaster of highs and lows. The good moments were great, and the bad times were just as unforgettable. The Christmas of my sophomore year at UCLA was the worst. Quite a few of the students came from the area around the university, so they went home for the holidays. Those of us who stayed behind were transferred to the two dorms that remained open.

The campus became a ghost town with just a few of us left to haunt it. Pasarell went home that year, and the only close friend who stayed behind was Jean Baker. There was no meal service for several days and I was flat broke. For the first time since I left home, I did not have a cent in my pocket.

J. D. invited me to his house for Christmas dinner, but I declined. Christmas is a family affair, and I knew I would feel like an intruder in his home, so I said, "No thanks, I've already made arrangements." But I really had no plans and I was too proud to ask my father to send me some money.

I was really depressed. Going from the opulence of the

J. D.

Racquet Club in Palm Springs to the loneliness of a penniless Christmas heightened my depression. I borrowed a dollar from Jean and bought some fruit and a sandwich from the vending machines in the basement of the dormitory on Christmas night. Fortunately, the cafeteria was only closed that one day, but the experience gave me a sober regard for money. Even five dollars would have meant I could walk to Westwood and see a movie. I wasn't tempted to run out and steal anything, but I thought long and hard about what it meant to have no money at all for an extended period. I was determined never to be in that situation again; now I find it difficult to say no to friends who want to borrow money.

Jeanne says that I'm more willing to do something if I feel I'm doing it for someone else and not myself. But one of my biggest virtues is patience. I'm a patient person even if my tennis game was the perfect foil to my personality. I'm not easily fooled. I may come out on the short end of the stick, but it's not because I didn't know any better. For example, I've loaned money to people—in some cases quite a bit of money. When someone says to me, "Gee, I need five hundred or a thousand dollars and I'll pay you back," chances are I won't get the money back. It's happened several times, even with friends.

One friend said he needed $500 to pay for some emergency surgery for his kid. He had no place to turn. I gave him the money and never got it back. I never asked for it and didn't get upset about it either. As far as I was concerned, once I gave him money, I figured I'd never see it again. If I do, I'm pleasantly surprised.

On another occasion, a black girl I had encouraged to attend law school said she needed $1,000. I wasn't looking for the money because I suspected she would need it to finish school and start a career, but she paid me back.

In April of '63, Charlie Pasarell and I were invited by Frank Feltrop, the pro at the California Club, to play an exhibition for some of the members. As we were leaving, a gentle, well-dressed, and very determined white woman came up to me. "Arthur, I certainly enjoyed your tennis out there today," she said. "What are your plans?"

I took her for another interested spectator, but her friendliness seemed genuine. "Ah, I don't know," I stammered. "If I can find the money, I'll go to Wimbledon next month. If not, I'll try to go back East and play the summer circuit there." I had won the Southern California sectional title and was eligible to play Wimbledon, which I had heard so much about.

"How much will it cost for Wimbledon?" she asked.

"Oh, about eight hundred dollars would do it."

"Well," she went on. "I certainly think you deserve a chance. Wait here just a moment, will you? I'll be right back."

I assumed she was going to get a business card. She walked about thirty yards down a long hall into a card room and shut the door behind her. About three minutes later, she came striding back and put eight crisp hundred-dollar bills in my hand.

"Here, this should do it," she said. "Good luck. We'll be looking for your name in the *Times*."

I was so stunned I could barely stammer my thanks. No one other than my father or Dr. Johnson had done anything like that for me. My heart was pounding as I tried to take control of myself. The money would enable me to play outside the country for the first time. I learned later that the lady was Mrs. Joan Ogner, wife of an automobile dealer in Beverly Hills. She had gone into the card room, found eight guys around the table, and hit each one for a hundred dollars. They probably never knew what she had done with the money.

Her act of kindness was very matter-of-fact. But for me, it balanced the Balboa Club incident, which had shattered my image of California. Now I knew there were warm and generous people out there who would give me a hand when they could.

The money could stretch that far because the NCAA tournament that year was held at Princeton. UCLA gave me an LA-NY-LA ticket, so all I had to do was buy a round-trip to London from New York. Robert Kelleher, another good friend, had been appointed Davis Cup captain that year. He promised J. D. to "look after" me while I was in London. He even helped arrange a second tournament in Budapest the week after Wimbledon.

The NCAAs turned out to be a replay of our dual match with USC earlier in the spring. Once again, we came in second for the team title. I faced Dennis Ralston in the semifinals and he again showed that he was simply a better player. He had a powerful game, even on Princeton's slow clay courts and won, 6–2, 8–6, 5–7, 3–6, 6–1. He went on and won the individual title by beating Osuna.

That same night, it seemed that almost everybody from the two teams was on the plane to London. Even without winning the NCAAs, I was flying on several levels.

The Initiation

London is my favorite city, and not simply because it was the first foreign city I visited. It appears to me the most civilized city in the world. Things work there. People are friendly. The British have a very deep sense of fairness despite their class consciousness. All Englishmen are snobs no matter what their status is in life, but they are patient and will "queue" for anything. My first glimpse of the "Wimbledon mystique" was the sight of people lining up for tickets. Until then, I thought baseball games and concerts were the only SRO events.

Changes in nomenclature also give London a distinct character. Elevator becomes "lift"; subways are "tubes." The warmup before a match was a "knock-up," a phrase that always drew laughs from American players.

"You Yanks have turned everything around again, haven't you? You even drive on the wrong side of the road," said the one-armed "lift" operator of the Westbury Hotel, where I stayed. I got to know him pretty well that first summer, and he gave me a tip on the horses every day. I could tell by his mood whether he had won or lost and listened respectfully to his advice; but in those days, I could hardly afford to bet or gamble.

As much as I love London, I developed a sensitivity there that would apply to every large city I visited. Wherever I go, I want to know who does what and specifically, what black people do there. I quickly found that in London, like Richmond, black people did the dirty work. The first thing I saw at Heathrow Airport after my arrival were the Indian and Pakistani women who cleaned the floor. West Indians and Asians swept the streets. But I never saw a black face among the famous Guards who change posts every morning for tourists at 11:30. In England, black people always appeared to be bystanders. Andrew Young, the former United States ambassador to the United Nations, was severely criticized for his remark that the British "institutionalized racism." If they didn't, how did it spread so far through the Commonwealth? The class system only made racism more oppressive.

I've had many black Britons stop me in the street to tell me how their families have been blocked from immigrating to England; how they can't live where they want; how they never get promoted; how the Labour party won't put up a black candidate in overwhelmingly black districts of London. There are no black MP's.

London reminded me of home in many ways, but Wimbledon is in a class by itself. The courts at Wimbledon are laid out roughly in a north-south direction. On those intermittently sunny English summer days, the sun passes in a parabola low in the sky from northeast to northwest. Any right-handed player will attest to the sun standing in his line of sight at 2 P.M., the traditional Wimbledon starting time. Because London is at 52 degrees north latitude, the sun doesn't set until 9:30 P.M. in the summer. That explains Wimbledon's starting time, but I never got to like it.

Wimbledon is a London suburb; the tennis facility is the All-England Lawn Tennis and Croquet Club, and the setting is similar to an Ivy League school, with ivy on the majestic brick walls surrounding Centre Court, on the old brick chapel down by Court 16, and on the sides of the concrete stands on the west side of Court 2. All of the courts have numbers and a certain history to them.

Every new male player at Wimbledon is ushered into the "B" locker room. Where there's a "B," there's an "A" in the British class system. The lesser-known players—the nobodies and qualifiers—were put in the "B" changing room. The British consider "locker room" a vulgar term, so there are no locks on the cabinets in either changing room.

In those days players were picked up in Rolls-Royces or Bentleys provided by wealthy club members and friends. I'll never forget my first ride in a Bentley: it was the roomiest car I had ever been in and the driver addressed me as "sir" or "mister." I was impressed, but not fooled. I had learned early to be wary of strangers or whites bearing gifts. Still, I enjoyed the luxury; it made me feel important even though I wasn't.

I didn't like the "B" locker room and still don't. It reminds me of the "separate but equal" cry of Virginia's *Massive Resistance* movement after the Brown decision. In fact, at Wimbledon, there was no attempt to disguise the inequalities of the two changing rooms. The message was clear: the superior amenities of the "A" rooms accrue to those who earn them. It wasn't segregation of a permanent sort; if one became a good player—a somebody— then you could move to the "A" rooms. After all, the "A" room was located beneath Centre Court.

My first match at Wimbledon was against Carlos Fernandes of Brazil. We met on Court 4, which is located in the first row of field courts. I'd never heard of Carlos, but since he was Brazilian I assumed he was pretty good on clay and not so hot on grass, because there aren't any grass courts in Brazil.

"Bon dia," Carlos said, in the "B" locker room before the match.

"What?" I answered.

"Bon dia." My blank stare finally told him I didn't understand. "Good morning," he said in perfect English.

"Oh, good morning. Fine, thanks. How are you?"

On an international circuit like tennis, it helps to master a few phrases in five or six languages. Once the niceties are over, however, it's out to the court. Carlos couldn't play on grass and couldn't handle my serve-and-volley game. I

74

overwhelmed him in straight sets and moved to the second round against John Hillebrand, an Aussie who got into the tournament by qualifying at Roehampton the week before Wimbledon. It had been expected that I would meet another Australian, John Newcombe, in what was being billed as a battle of promising junior players. But Newcombe defaulted to Hillebrand, and I beat Hillebrand in five sets.

Suddenly, in my first Wimbledon, I had reached the third round. I was so excited and nervous I could hardly contain myself. The first win over Fernandes had been the psychological hump. Wimbledon had grass courts like Forest Hills, but the name and importance of the tournament put an added burden on many players. For me, moving to the next round was like my first big win over one of those "white boys" on the junior circuit.

Every evening on the first trip, a group of us would walk up Conduit Street to Regent, turn right and walk half a mile to the little statue of Eros in the center of Picadilly Circus. We ate dinner at a Lyons Corner House and roamed Soho. The pilgrimage to the heart of London became a habit, and even now I have a hard time resisting the stroll to pay homage to Eros whenever I'm in London.

My third-round opponent that first year was Chuck McKinley, the No. 1 American player. We met on Court 6, next to the canvas-covered "members' enclosure." It is the noisiest court at Wimbledon because the members are talking, eating, and drinking right next to the court. But I couldn't blame the members for my game against McKinley. He was the best U.S. player, and I was talented but inexperienced. He beat me in straight sets and went on to win the tournament without losing a set.

In the years that followed, my top-ten cities emerged rather clearly. After London, they were Hong Kong, Paris, Rome, Venice, Rio de Janeiro, Monte Carlo, Perth, Singapore, and Stockholm.

Arthur Ashe: OFF THE COURT

From England, I flew to Budapest and a tournament on St. Margaret's Island in the middle of the Danube. I didn't get much expense money (always a concern in the days before pro tennis), but the tournament was important in enhancing my reputation. (I had received £50 in expenses at Wimbledon while the top players and Davis Cuppers got 100.) The two stars at Budapest were Istvan Gulyas, a Hungarian who was one of the world's best clay players, and Torben Ulrich, a very individualistic Dane. I made it to the semifinals and lost in five sets to Torben.

The summer of '63 led to a very good year for me. I made the cover of *World Tennis* magazine in November for the first time and finished as the sixth-ranked player in the country. I also was selected to the Davis Cup team. Besides the prestige there were numerous advantages to playing Davis Cup. As a team member, I would be entitled to £100 in expenses at Wimbledon the following year and also would escape the "B" lockers. The opportunities for travel shaped many of my ideas.

I take a little longer making decisions than most people. But when I make a decision, it's done; I don't second-guess. Every once in a while, I may get impulsive and make a decision without thinking of all the ramifications. A few years ago, I bought a 1924 Rolls-Royce Silver Ghost for $55,000 that I saw in a showroom in Australia.

"It's a rather expensive impulse you got there," Jeanne teased after I bought the car, but I just fell in love with it; I've only driven it twice, both times in Australia, and I keep it at my father's house—but I love old things. I even collect walking sticks. I bought one stick at an antique show at Park Avenue and Sixty-first Street for $80 and another in Venice that cost $200. If Jeanne and I go for a walk, I'll take a walking stick with me. I don't know the significance, but I get a kick out of it.

Once I've made up my mind about something, I approach it calmly, usually because I've done considerable research. For example, there's a great deal of ignorance about sex in the United States, even though it is our major preoccupation in one form or another throughout the world. I could ask ten of my closest male friends, black and white, to explain the menstrual cycle to me and maybe one or two could do it. There seems to be a Calvinistic attitude toward sex in this country; it's a subject that should be discussed in the home, but seldom is. I read Masters and Johnson's *Human Sexual Response* and *Human Sexual Inadequacies* from cover to cover because I wanted to learn how scientific principles relate to real life experiences.

There has always been considerable speculation about the effect of sex on athletic performance. I think it's a question of who you have sex with. If you're married or have a long-time girl friend and you make love for twenty minutes the night before some match but still sleep eight hours, there's no problem. But if you are up half the night, or you're a single guy (or girl) who has been out until two in the morning looking for something, that's got to hurt you. The body can't take too much of that.

I wasn't worried that much, because I looked at sex very scientifically. For a man it takes about ninety calories to perform the average sex act. If you want to relieve tension before a match and you take fifteen minutes, even if it's the night before, it won't mean a damn thing as far as your sport is concerned. It might affect you psychologically if you think it does. But in actual fact, Masters and Johnson did some studies with people trying to perform complicated physical tasks at various stages after sex, and the differences weren't that significant. A lot depends on who it's with: if it's a regular partner, no problem; if it's with somebody new, it's much more stimulating, and it takes more energy. The freshness of it all may have more lasting effects.

There always were, always are, and always will be tennis

groupies on the pro tour. That shouldn't surprise any-body—least of all the wives of male tennis players. The same situation applies to the other sports as well. But be-cause I once had an affair with a married woman, I am much less holier-than-thou about indiscretions. When I started out on the men's tour at nineteen years of age, players never traveled with girlfriends. Today, that sort of arrangement is common.

Jeanne and I will hear about the occasional indiscretion on the tour. Though neither of us condones such activity, talking about it is cathartic for both of us. We are old-fashioned enough to live by rules of fidelity, respect, and compassion. Yet we are modern enough to understand a live-in arrangement or a player traveling the circuit with his girlfriend. The ultimate test of course is: Would we approve of our daughter doing it? Probably not. We allow each other quite a bit of freedom. Life is difficult enough as it is without complicating matters. Naturally, if I look too long at some woman, I'm sure to get an elbow in the ribs.

Several years ago on the Richmond stop of the tour, Buster Mottram was chatting with this very striking crea-ture just outside the Coliseum. Buster pulled out all the stops as he offered tickets to the matches and maybe din-ner later. Getting positive responses, Buster pressed on, and before long they were back at his hotel for a quick drink and then up to his room. Within ten minutes of entering his room, Buster came screaming down the hall-way as white as an English country girl in the dead of winter. "It's a man; it's a man," he kept screaming. Seems that the girl he thought he was about to score with was a boy.

The most serious moral issue I encountered at UCLA dealt with the most forbidden fruit of all—white women. When I got to UCLA, my experience with women had been limited. I've heard that men's relationships with women are based on associations with their mothers, but my mother had died when I was six.

In my travels, I learned there is no such thing as a "universal" choice in the opposite sex. I was exposed to all sizes, shapes and colors of black women as a child—in school, in church, in my own family. I learned quickly that hazel eyes, straight hair, and light skin were preferred. At seven years old, I did not see anything wrong with that. Everyone I knew thought that way. Most black people seemed conditioned to accept these characteristics as normal standards of beauty, even if such conditions were unfair.

My mother was referred to in our community as "brown-skinned." She wasn't high yellow and she wasn't very dark. She had brown, not hazel eyes. Her hair was somewhere between "straight" and "kinky."

I noticed that little black girls (and their mothers) went to great pains to straighten their hair. When I looked up "hair" in my encyclopedia, I was startled by the explanations of different hair types. The pictures showed cross-sections of Oriental, Caucasian, and Negro hair. Negro hair was shaped like a bent soda straw, which caused it to curl. The flatter the hair, the more it curled.

The logic of why black women suffered over hair seemed terribly unfair, but the typical black woman had no place in the Western pantheon of beauty. The whole thing confused me, as it did generations of black Americans.

I had no real romantic attachments in grade school, and sexual urges didn't begin to appear until the ninth grade. I was attracted to the physical woman, not her personality. I developed crushes on teachers like Miss Alston at Maggie Walker and Mrs. Lee, who taught math at B. A. Graves Junior High. I would sit and stare for hours at Mrs. Lee —furtively, of course.

Arthur Ashe: OFF THE COURT

My first sexual experience happened almost by accident. I was a junior at Maggie Walker and had had my driver's license for about a year. Coming home from a party in the West End of Richmond, I offered to drive three friends home in my father's car. I dropped a couple off and found myself alone with a girl I didn't know very well.

We decided to double back to Byrd Park and visit the fountain, which changed colors every ten seconds. As we approached, we saw that several other cars were already parked around the fountain, so we decided to find a more isolated place deeper inside the park. It was a nice night. After the usual small talk, we started kissing and petting. One thing led to another, but the young lady was definitely in charge. She tugged at my pants and zipper. She said she had seen me play JV basketball and tennis but was told "hands off." My girlfriend at the time was Saundra Scott.

"Saundra ain't here now and she won't know if you don't tell her," she said. "I'm sure not going to tell her."

Soon my pants were down, her dress was up and her panties pulled down and she shoved me under the steering wheel. I just went along. At this point, I was putting on an Academy Award performance. Afterward, I acted as cool as Paul Newman in *Cool Hand Luke* because I could not let her think this was my first time. She seemed to have enjoyed it, because we kissed some more, rolled the window down to get rid of the fog inside, and took a short walk around the carillon in the park. After I took her home, I began to think about the risk we had taken in the park. What if we had been caught? Of course, the whole thing happened in fifteen minutes, but I kept thinking about the dangers. I hadn't seen a police car while we were in Byrd Park. Weeks later, I casually brought up the subject of police with my father.

"Don't they patrol Byrd Park at night?" I asked. "I've gone by there a couple of times and I've never seen any police cars."

"Oh, they're there," my father assured me. "You don't see them because they use unmarked cars—quite a few of them."

Because I lived in a segregated society, all my friends in Virginia were black. I came into contact with girls of other races when I began spending my summers with Dr. Johnson. Most of the junior events were coed, but there were few occasions to get to know white girls very well.

When I was fifteen, I met Patricia Battles of Stamford, Connecticut, at one of the ATA events. She was the daughter of one of the black teaching pros, and I flipped over her. She had smooth light brown skin, brown eyes, brown wavy hair, and a great figure. She was Catholic. We saw each other whenever we could at summer tournaments. From the time I was fifteen, we wrote to each other and dated off and on. My crush on Pat Battles lasted eight years, through my years at UCLA and all my girlfriends in between.

We got engaged in 1966 and set a wedding date for June of the following year. After I graduated from UCLA and arrived at West Point for duty there, White Plains, where she now lived, was only forty minutes away. We decided to go to the Caribe Hilton Tennis Tournament in San Juan during my leave in March 1967. We took separate rooms and planned to have a nice week while I played the tournament. But I began to have second thoughts about getting married at twenty-four. By that time, I had made trips to Australia and Europe and played Davis Cup matches abroad. My father was all for the marriage; her folks liked me. Yet, I decided to call it off. Pat took it all rather calmly, more calmly than I did. I felt ashamed of the breakup and wondered how a business decision could make me fall out of love. For a long time, I thought I was rather cold-blooded about it, but the trips abroad had opened up new worlds and I wanted to see and experience those without the burden of a wife and possibly children. As time went by, I realized it had been the right decision.

Arthur Ashe: OFF THE COURT

I caused considerable embarrassment for both of us, but it was probably better than an unhappy marriage. Later, neither of us regretted it. Pat is now happily married and the mother of four children.

A black man could have gotten killed for dating a white woman in Richmond in the 1950s. Society there wouldn't stand for interracial dating, let alone interracial marriage. There were even several antimiscegenation laws on the books in Virginia. UCLA was another story. As a freshman living in a coed dorm, I was surrounded by girls from everywhere. The atmosphere was definitely anything goes.

I met a young woman whom I will call Phyllis Jones at a dance in the dorm one night. She was absolutely stunning, with coal-black hair, a tight green skirt, and dark green turtleneck sweater. And white. I was unable to take my eyes off her. She caught me looking at her and stared back boldly.

You must understand that a southern boy who played tennis was teased about white women by other black athletes. California was much freer about racial matters than Virginia, or any other southern state, for that matter. As I stood there, the combination of emotions and thoughts about my next step nearly froze me in place. After twenty minutes of glances across the dance floor, I summoned enough nerve to go over and mumble the usual, "Hello. What's your name?" It turned out she was a friend of a friend. I asked her to dance. I had never danced with a white girl before.

After a while, we went out on the patio to talk. We talked for three hours. From there, you could look eastward and get a good view of the campus. We stopped only because she had to get back to the dorm before the 2 A.M. lock-out time. We pecked each other on the cheek and agreed to see each other again.

Talk about old southern taboos coming back to haunt you. I was scared, thrilled, excited, sweating and numb—

all at the same time. The fact that she was different was part of my attraction to her. Each of us brought our own perceptions and life experiences to UCLA. We tried to mix and reconcile, probe and experiment with our differing values and judgments. I don't think many of my white classmates ever dated a black woman. When you're in the majority, you don't feel you have to make any accommodation. Assimilation, if any, is for the minority. So is experimentation. Those in dominance don't need it; they can be satisfied with the status quo. For someone like me, from the small stifling world of Richmond, the opportunity to try something new—unknown and forbidden— could not be squandered.

She told her mother about me and that I played on the UCLA tennis team. At first, I worried about what my family would think, what J. D. would think. But everyone that mattered was so far away. I talked to Susan Ikei. She thought I was dumb to worry so much.

One day my picture appeared on Los Angeles television and Phyllis's mother saw me. She was devastated. "You didn't tell me he was a Negro!" she screamed at her. "I don't ever want him in my house, do you hear?" Phyllis had left out one important fact about me because she suspected her mother would not take kindly to our relationship. We continued to see each other for several months and developed a good rapport. Like all novelties, however, she wore off. I was learning that women were women and they were all different.

So was the mystique of the black athlete. If you were in sports at UCLA, no matter which one, you were considered pretty good. Some women thought that a good athlete was also probably good in bed. This fascination with sexual excellence was a powerful force. Most black athletes could have any woman they wanted, black or white. Some ethnic groups were more difficult to penetrate: the Asians and Mexican-Americans, for instance.

The black women at UCLA clearly did not like the idea of black males dating white women, even if they thought they were better than the black males.

Once you went away from Westwood, California, with a white woman, however, the situation changed. I had never been stared at like that before, as if I was doing something morally wrong. At one point, I called my father and asked what he thought if I were to have a white wife.

"Don't make no difference to me," he said. "As long as she's a good person." Even over the long-distance line, his matter-of-fact tone came through clearly. Of course, I was only nineteen at the time.

I believe that interracial dating helps different people to learn about each other. I learned about Asians from dating Asians. I learned about Jews from Jewish girlfriends. What bothered me in later years was that I somehow fell for women in impossible situations even as I felt freer from convention and self-doubt.

For example, I had an affair with a married woman once, not out of curiosity but because we inadvertently began to like each other. Ours was primarily a telephone love affair, with occasional letters and rare secret rendezvous. The unavoidable breakup was filled with tension and I suffered through several months of guilt, but I knew I had to take my share of the responsibility for what I had been doing all along.

In 1972, I entered a tournament in Teheran. I had never played in a Moslem country and the Aryemehr Cup at the Imperial Country Club seemed to be a good opportunity. I met a Persian woman there who just freaked me out. She was beautiful, with long, flowing, black hair, and she spoke Farsi, French, Arabic, and English flawlessly. She had never met a black man, although at first glance many Iranians resemble light-skinned black Americans.

She hated the Shah. Some of her friends and classmates had just "disappeared," perhaps because of political expediency. At the same time, she realized her family's good life was due to the Shah. One day after my match, we took a ride to the countryside about thirty miles from Teheran and I could see that life for women was much worse in the villages. It reminded me of African villages where women seemed to do all the work. In the Iranian villages, the women were all veiled. Only their eyes peeked through.

She took me everywhere. We visited the Crown Jewels Museum and the famous Bazaar; and we ate caviar every afternoon in the lobby of the Hilton. At night, we danced at La Cheminée, the "in" disco of Teheran at the time. But while we lived in a westernized way, there were reminders of the dominant Moslem culture. As we were riding in a taxi one day, I leaned over to kiss her. She wanted to reciprocate but hesitated for a second before leaning toward me. The taxi came to a screeching halt. The driver, peering in the rear-view mirror, turned around and started shouting at her in Farsi. She looked embarrassed. "Kissing and showing affection in public is forbidden," she explained.

Her downcast look turned to defiance. "I don't care," she said boldly. "That is a stupid law anyway. This country is so backward!"

"Why didn't you tell him you weren't Persian and didn't know the Moslem law?" I asked later.

"He could tell," she answered, "and women aren't anything here anyway. I hope my father lets me leave here soon—forever. It's either leave Persia or Savak may take me away for something."

I was pained not to see her more often. We saw each other later at Wimbledon and went to Valencia for a memorable weekend. Since the fall of the Shah, I've tried more than once to find out if she is still alive or in Teheran—but without success; I suspect that she may have been right up there in the street demonstrations during the recent uprisings.

My quasi-celebrity status in later years gave me access to

some very "glamorous" women. During Wimbledon in 1974, Diana Ross was in London, heard I was playing in the tournament, and called me. Her record company drove her out to Wimbledon in a burgundy Rolls-Royce; we met in the foyer and went up to the players' tea room. I had already played and won my match that afternoon. When she walked into the room, all eyes turned to us. We spent a pleasant afternoon watching some of the matches from the roof of the Tea Room.

Diana was a very poised woman who had made it from the projects of Detroit to stardom. I thought we made an odd couple as we sat in the back of her Rolls on our way to the Mayfair Hotel, where she was staying. We had a few drinks together, but she had a dinner engagement and was leaving for Los Angeles the following morning. We arranged to meet again in two weeks in Washington. I was going to play in the *Washington Star* tournament and she would be performing at the Carter Baron Amphitheater next door. It turned out that we unknowingly were on the same floor of the Washington Hilton and had dinner together on a couple of evenings. One night, my family came up from Richmond with some home-cooked food and we all ate in her suite. She seemed lonely at the time and really enjoyed the warmth of the family gathering.

Beverly Johnson was another story. Her face has graced the covers of every major fashion magazine. I thought her photographs were stunning, had wanted to meet her for some time, and kept asking Gene Barakat, a New Zealander who worked at the Ford modeling agency, "When are you going to introduce me to Beverly Johnson?"

"As soon as she's free and in town," he would reply.

On a scale of 1 to 10, Beverly is a 9. She must be one of the three most beautiful women I ever dated. We hit it off right away. On our first date, we went to see *The Wiz* on Broadway. I was a bit stunned when an autograph seeker approached us as we neared the theater and asked for

The Initiation

Beverly's autograph first. That had never happened to me before. I had never dated anyone as well known, except for Diana Ross. The modeling business is a bit like tennis. I was the only top black player and she was clearly the top black model, at least until Iman came along. I don't think I ever felt so scrutinized as when I went out with her. She came to visit me in Boston and at Forest Hills. Although I never went to one of her jobs, we talked a great deal about her profession.

Even without makeup, Beverly was stunning. She had almost perfect bone structure, smooth dark skin, no blemishes. She loved a good time and a party, which was fine because I wasn't especially a party type. My idea of a good time was a good book, a little Bartok, or great conversation.

Beverly had trouble finding guys who were not after her money. "I'm young, beautiful, rich, and black and that's a problem sometimes," she once said to me. But my travel schedule took me away and our contact was gradually reduced to telephone calls and then even less.

If my life changed as a result of travel, in ways I could not have imagined as a youngster reading *National Geographic*s on the back porch of our house in Richmond, blacks were also discovering a new assertiveness. They no longer feared "whitey," or worried about the Klan. New voices began to challenge the value of nonviolence. Leaders like Malcolm X, H. Rap Brown, and Stokely Carmichael articulated the anger blacks felt over brothers and sisters being beaten, shot, and jailed. The 1964 riots in Harlem spread to Rochester, Newark, and then Watts.

People have said to me, "Well, you were in Los Angeles, couldn't you see Watts coming?" But I didn't know Los Angeles, even after several years. Most of my life out West was spent at UCLA. Whenever I went any place into black Los Angeles, it was usually to my fraternity house on Crenshaw Boulevard, not to Watts. I didn't know anybody who lived there, so I had no reason to go. Watts held no special social significance then; it only gained significance after the riots. In fact, Compton had a stronger black identity for many Californians than Watts at the time. If I had gone to Watts I would have been like the New Yorkers who go to Little Italy—it's usually just to eat lunch or dinner, not to study the sociology of the place.

Discrimination is not limited to white-American prejudice against blacks. For example, after several trips to Europe, I noticed that central and northern Europeans tend to turn up their noses at southern Europeans. In Australia, the problems among Greek and Italian immigrants and white Australians are similar to those between the white Australians and the Aborigines. The Greeks and Italians living in Australia would tell me, "These Australians are lazy, they don't want to work. We're building all these buildings, we do all the masonry, all the bricklaying." In Italy and Greece, these same people might have been nobodies, but because the Australian government paid for them to come to Australia because of their skills, they became bigshots.

I get irritated with the attitudes of foreign cab drivers in Washington, D.C., or New York. One day, Mike Estep and I took a cab to practice in Manhattan. I like to engage in conversation with cab drivers because maybe I'll learn something new. I found out that this cabbie was Armenian and had been in the United States about four months.

"I have to pick up a package at this apartment," I told the cabbie, while we were on our way to the practice court. "I'd like you to wait for a minute."

"I don't wanna wait," the cabbie said.

His response irritated me. "You have to wait," I said. "If you don't, I won't pay you. And if you don't like it, you can go to a policeman. So you'll just wait until I get back. I'm coming right back." Mike was in the back seat with me.

The cabbie said he would not wait. I was burning, so I

told him, "Look, it's this simple: if you don't like it, go find a policeman and let's have it out." So he waited. But here was a guy who had been in my country four months telling me he didn't want to wait. I could understand that from someone who had been here for years, just as I always understood the centuries-old antagonism between Christians and Jews. I wasn't trying to cheat him out of his fare. He just didn't want to lose money by waiting in the taxi. He was in the United States because things are better here than they were in his country, yet he was already trying to go one-up on everyone any way he could, without any regard for the benefits that were coming his way.

At this time my own political views were evolving. I disagreed with some of the methods of Malcolm X and others, and Martin Luther King, Jr., and Andrew Young had joined Joe Louis and Jackie Robinson in my hall of heroes. I was particularly fascinated by Andy Young long before we ever met; I identified with him. He was a conciliator committed to the cause, someone who could haggle, bargain, and win compromises with whites. I wondered what gifts enabled him to play this role so well. I was not yet ready to play such an active political role; but in a vague, unspoken way, I felt myself wanting to open up more and more about the way our society operated.

The politics of the time dictated an even more important and immediate personal decision. At UCLA, all underclassmen had to take two years of ROTC. After your sophomore year, I had to decide if I wanted to take two more years, which involved a commitment to military service after graduation. I talked about "going ROTC all the way" with my father. He liked the idea of me becoming an officer. J. D. and Bob Kelleher, a Beverly Hills lawyer who was the new Davis Cup captain, had a different reason for suggesting I complete the program—the war in Vietnam.

My family had a history of military involvement. My uncle Rudy Cunningham was once in the Marines, my

89

brother Johnny is a Marine officer, and several uncles were in the Navy. My concern was that I was 1-A and would surely be drafted after graduation.

I met with Kelleher and J. D. There wasn't much anti-war fever in 1963, so there was no strong political issue. "You would be better off going in as an officer than an enlisted man," advised J. D., who had been a PT boat commander in World War II.

"An officer's commission would look good on any re-sume," Kelleher reasoned.

J. D. was not worried about Charlie Pasarell, Dave Reed, or the other players. They came from well-to-do families and could take care of themselves. He was concerned about my situation. It wasn't a bad decision to go with the army. And life after college would have some objectives, so I signed up.

In my final years at UCLA, I won the NCAA singles and doubles title in 1965 while making friends with a broad range of people; some were tennis players, some were classmates. As a black tennis player, I was somewhat iso-lated as black athletes go. There was only one other good black tennis player in the Pac-8 Conference, Doug Sykes at Cal-Berkeley. He was probably the second-best black player in the country in those years. When we saw each other, we joked about being tokens, but he played a lower number on his team and we never met on the court.

The only other Third World tennis players I ran into regularly were Alex Olmedo and Pancho Segura. Olmedo, a full-blooded Inca Indian from Peru, played for USC and represented the U.S. Davis Cup team in 1958 and 1959. Pancho also came from predominantly Indian stock, in Ecuador. He always referred to Gonzales, Alex Olmedo, himself, and me as the "brown bodies." When I won Wim-bledon in 1975 he came up to me and said, "Ah ha, the brown bodies are doing much better, I see."

Charles Rombeau bridged my childhood and years at UCLA. Chuck was the left-handed player from Studio

City whom I beat for my first big win over "one of those white boys" when I was fifteen years old. He and I became friends because we played the juniors together and went to Los Angeles schools on scholarships. He was the No. 6 player at USC. We traveled to tournaments together and then he started to have nervous fits. We all thought he had contracted epilepsy. Once, on a long trip from Los Angeles to Phoenix, he slept half the time and wasn't in full control of himself the rest of the time.

Chuck's father was a doctor, and somehow I assumed that if something was seriously wrong it would be taken care of. But Chuck's sickness progressed, became more debilitating, and he spent several months completely doped up. Eventually, he died of a brain tumor. We all wondered if he would have survived if the correct diagnosis had been made earlier.

I had no serious physical ailments. But once, after playing at the La Jolla Beach and Tennis Club in a suburb of San Diego, Charlie Pasarell and I decided to go down to nearby Tijuana for the evening with a few other friends. Charlie was seated next to me in the backseat, looked up and read a sign out loud, "Tijuana seventeen miles."

"How can you see that?" I asked.

"There's the sign," he said.

I could see the sign but couldn't make out the lettering.

"You need glasses, Ashe," Charlie said.

Sure enough, I had never been to an eye doctor in my life. When I got back to Los Angeles, I had my eyes examined. The doctor said my eyes were "significantly off" and prescribed a pair of glasses. I walked out of his office and jumped for joy. I never realized that I had been living in a blur, and I was actually high for a couple of days from the excitement of seeing everything so clearly. The glasses didn't have much effect on my tennis, but I had to adjust to the sharper and smaller images. Once I did, my confidence improved considerably.

I played my first Davis Cup match in 1963. We already

had beaten Iran and Mexico that year and were ahead, 3–0, in the series against Venezuela at the Cherry Hill Country Club in Denver. So with nothing to lose, Kelleher let me play a meaningless singles match on the final day against Orlando Bracamonte. I won, 6–1, 6–1, 6–0. With Chuck McKinley, Dennis Ralston, and Frank Froehling available in those days, however, it would be almost two years before I would play another Davis Cup match.

In the mid-sixties, the Davis Cup existed under a so-called Challenge Round system. The team that won the competition one year did not have to play through the draw the following year, only defend its title in the Challenge Round. Ralston and McKinley beat the Aussies, 3–2, in Adelaide in 1963, so the U.S. had only one match in 1964. We lost to Australia this time, 3–2 in Cleveland, in the Challenge Round when Fred Stolle beat Ralston, 7–5, 6–3, 3–6, 9–11, 6–4, in the key fifth match.

Ralston led Stolle, 3–1, in the fifth set. But Harry Hopman, the foxy Aussie captain, told Fred to "go for the lines." Fred did, and the Aussies were rolling in Foster's beer that night.

Hopman was the main reason for the success of Australian tennis in those days. When he left Australia and moved to the United States, Australian domination of tennis died. Hopman was one of the first coaches who saw the value of taking good athletes and making them great tennis players. There's no question that today's players are better than the stars of the sixties. The reason is because they're better athletes. Back then only Australia had great athletes who played tennis. The rest of us, including myself, tried to make the best of our talent. If I could go back and take one-third of the players who are now playing for the National Basketball Association when they were just ten, there's no question in my mind that I could produce superior tennis players, on the level of a Bjorn Borg and John McEnroe. Guys like John Lucas and Calvin Murphy would be unbelievable tennis players because they possess great lateral movement, quickness and endurance—the skills that are required in tennis. Borg played hockey before he moved into tennis. McEnroe was a soccer player in high school even while he was refining his serve and volley.

The only thing that I would worry about with players like a Randy Smith or Walt Frazier is that they might put too much flair into their games. As good an athlete as Ilie Nastase is—and he's a good one with his touch and coordination—there are some guys in the NBA who could run circles around Nastase. And Randy Smith is just as quick as Borg.

Hopman was the predecessor to the modern coaches who travel with players today. If I had come along later, I would have availed myself of a coach. A good one can pick up subtleties in a player's game that the player takes for granted. With so much prize money up for grabs now, players need all the help they can get. If a coach can bring out the best, it pays for the player to utilize that service. But not every coach suits each player. Ion Tiriac, for example, may be perfect for Guillermo Vilas, but his strong-mindedness would be deadly for Bjorn Borg. Nick Bollettieri has won a reputation for developing the will to win in players and in the conditioning phase of the game. He seems to be good with somebody who has already gotten the basics down and needs to polish the rough edges. By contrast, Dennis Van Der Meer's approach is more institutional. He teaches the teachers how to run their clubs, conduct clinics, refine strokes. If I had to send my kid to somebody to learn from scratch, I would send him or her to Welby Van Horn. He has the best track record. I don't know if he still has the same enthusiasm, but he's turned out the champions. You don't do that by accident. Robert Lansdorp has to be right up there, too, now. Tracy Austin has a very, very sound game, and Lansdorp was good for her mental approach.

What helped me was the opportunity to travel and play

under different circumstances. In October 1965, after our Davis Cup team had been upset by Spain on slow clay courts in Barcelona, George McCall had replaced Vic Seixas as captain, decided to keep the team together for an entire year. Our first stops—New Zealand and Australia. With only one semester of school left, I decided to make the trip to Australia, graduate in the spring of 1966, and then begin my military obligation that summer.

New Zealand was the greenest place I'd ever seen, obviously because it rained a lot. We stayed with families or in hotels during our week there and played in Auckland, Christchurch, Dunedin, Invercargill, and Rotarua, a showy tourist spot with hot sulphur springs that are sacred to the Maoris.

Maoris are to New Zealand what the Aborigines are to Australia and the Indians to us. They were not especially tall people—just wide, the first South Sea Islanders I had ever seen. I looked at them and wondered, "Where the hell did they come from?" Of course, my curiosity would become more acute when I first met Fijians and Aborigines.

We decided to spend twenty-four hours on Fiji after New Zealand, and a wild twenty-four hours it was! Mosquito netting hung from our canopied beds. We rode into a sugar cane field and stopped to chop down a stalk. My first taste was an experience. When the green, hard cover was cut away, the firm, white pulp was sliced into sticks. I chewed the stick and the delicious liquid filled my mouth. After the juice was squeezed out, I spat out dry, fibrous pulp before taking another bite.

As we cruised through the field, Sally Riessen, then married to Marty, asked our guide, a Pan Am employee, to stop.

"I've lost a button on my dress," she wailed. "I'll never find another one like it."

The car screeched to a halt. We got out and backtracked

along the road, looking for Sally's button. While we were looking, an East Indian man rode up on a beautiful horse. I used to ride on Sunday mornings near Malibu, and the sight of this magnificent animal brought back the pleasure of those trots in the mountains.

"Could I ride your horse for a couple of minutes?" I asked.

"Are you nuts?" Jim McManus said.

The owner spoke no English. We negotiated by sign language and he seemed willing enough. There were a couple of English words in his vocabulary. "Very fast," he said, pointing to his horse. "Very fast, very fast."

"Great," I told him. My friends were now debating the wisdom of my actions, but my masculinity was on the line. I couldn't back out. I was barely aboard when the horse took off—and not in the direction I wanted to go. I didn't know that the owner and the horse were on their way home, and the horse was even more anxious to get there.

The situation became obvious very quickly. The horse was going much faster than I had ever gone back at the Twin Oaks Riding Stable, and nothing I could do was having the slightest effect. At thirty miles an hour my passport, tickets, and wallet flew out of my pockets. I held on, but the English saddle had no horn like the Western ones I was accustomed to. I would get killed if I didn't get off. I squeezed my legs against the horse's side to work my feet free of the stirrups. The pressure only made the horse gallop faster. As soon as my feet felt free, I jumped off the starboard or wrong side into a row of sugar cane. I landed on my side, bruised but unbroken. I had been scared, but there was no permanent injury. It would be a while before I went near another horse.

Australia turned out to be as important to my tennis career as meeting Dr. Johnson and living in St. Louis during my senior year in high school. I had my first opportunity to play on grass for three straight months and won my spurs as an international player. I won four tournaments, beating Roy Emerson in Brisbane and winning in Adelaide, Perth, and Hobart, Tasmania. I made it to the final in two others, losing the Australian title to Emerson.

My performance earned me rave reviews in Australia and back home. But I also learned that there were more interesting facets to a country than hitting balls back and forth across a net. I absorbed as much as I could about Australia. It was so far away. There was an obvious British influence in the customs and habits of the Aussies, influences imposed on a territory four-fifths the size of the United States with a population of 14 million. Australian cities reminded me of London transplanted to Southern California, but there was none of the English snottiness. The Australians were fiercely middle class and quick to put down any attempts at snobbishness or pretension.

Here too I was fascinated by their attitudes about race, which reminded me initially of my experiences in Virginia. The Aborigines, or "Abos," as the Australians called them, were among the most unusual people I had ever seen. They had a strange amalgam of racial characteristics: dark skin but straight hair, broad nostrils but razor-thin lips, slightly protruding buttocks, and very prominent foreheads. In talking to them, I learned they had many of the same problems black Americans were confronted with, but they compared themselves more to American Indians. "Aborigine" means native. They had been there long before the arrival of Captain Cook and had been decimated by the settlers from Europe. They numbered less than a million in a population of 14 million and had not been assimilated very well into the mainstream of Australia. Some of the Australian tennis players argued that they were lazy, didn't come to work on time, and didn't have any ambitions. It sounded too familiar. The white Australians seemed to have little understanding of the sociological problems faced by the Aborigines as they attempted to move from their ancient culture to a modern one.

I didn't spend all my time playing tennis or analyzing the country's sociological characteristics. I also explored Australian social life. Australian women seemed badly treated by their men. Founded by ex-convicts and misfits, Australia went through its own Wild West era. Women are kept firmly in "their place" by a traditional male chauvinism that has not yet been challenged. The idea of a date for some Australian men is to go to an RSL club and join their buddies at the bar for a few drinks while the women are off in a corner. By comparison, American men seem unusually gentle and solicitous.

I graduated from UCLA in June 1966, went directly to ROTC training camp in Fort Lewis, Washington, and was plunged immediately into the simplistic, disciplined, and physical world of the military. The summer camp was the equivalent of basic training for future officers. It had all the harassment and dehumanization which seem to be required ingredients for creating soldiers. But there was also a process of learning to take responsibility. Cadets held various ranks for limited periods of time to learn the different levels of the job.

On the first day, I was appointed deputy brigade commander. We hadn't gone fifteen yards beyond the gate when the cadet brigade commander stepped into a pothole and sprained an ankle. He had to be taken to the infirmary; suddenly I was in charge of an entire unit of eight hundred men. At the end of the day, I was told to take my troops back to the barracks and line them up in the courtyard so they could be dismissed. I had everybody fall in, gave the order to march and took them by the shortest route I could figure—down the road, through the gate, between a couple of buildings, and into the square.

Just as I was about to dismiss them, I realized the unit was lined up backward.

"You've really got it fucked up, mister," one of the training officers said. I had to take the brigade out again, turn them around, and bring them back the way they were supposed to be. I was terribly embarrassed because I was already in the spotlight over my tennis.

Somehow, I survived the next six weeks. I learned about weapons, tactics, map reading and other useful skills. I made good friends, earned my second-lieutenant's commission, and managed to play a few summer tournaments before my induction.

At Orange, New Jersey, that summer, I ran into Bill Cullen, the tennis and squash coach at West Point. Cullen asked about my induction and military school.

"We'd be interested in having you as an assistant tennis coach at the Point," he said.

I replied enthusiastically. "I'd have a chance to play most evenings," I said.

"We're going to need a data-processing officer," Cullen continued. "The two posts could be combined."

"What do I have to do?"

"Go to data-processing school. I'll take care of the rest."

During the next two years, I tried to combine my tennis and military careers. There were ups and downs on both ends. Our Davis Cup team was beaten in Brazil in 1966 and then suffered an even more embarrassing setback the following year, losing to Ecuador 3–2 at the Guayaquil Tennis Club. My losses to Miguel Olvera and Pancho Guzman in that series have to rank as one of the low points of my career, even though they came on clay.

During my last night in Ecuador, I got horribly sick and kept getting up to vomit. When I reported to the tennis stadium on Sunday morning, with our team trailing 2–1, I told George McCall about my condition. We had a team physician, a radiologist, who was a friend of George's from

Los Angeles. I had no choice but to get out on the court against Guzman. I didn't play well. I won the first set, 6–0, but lost the next two, 6–4, 7–5. I wasn't sure what I was doing out there.

During the intermission, George and I got pretty hot at each other. Our strategy wasn't working, and I didn't know what to do. He started punching lockers out of frustration. Cliff Richey realized that I needed some guidance.

"Look," Cliff said, "I'm going to tell you exactly what to do now. Go out there and don't miss a ball. Don't go for any winners. Just get the ball in the court and don't make any errors."

I did exactly what Cliff said and won the fourth set 6–0. But I wasn't sure what I should do next, so I figured I should pour it on. Not a very good idea. I lost 6–3, and the Ecuadorians went as wild as the Spaniards and Brazilians had done in 1965 and 1966.

I like George McCall immensely. He had the guts to select me for the Davis Cup against Mexico in 1965 when I was still an unproven player. And I had justified his faith by beating Rafe Osuna 6–2, 6–3, 9–7 in the opening match. We had become good friends, but George was an insurance broker at the time, not a tennis coach, and his appointment had been the result of tennis politics. Funny enough, he is now the Tennis Director at the Sands Hotel in Las Vegas.

By the end of 1967, I was ranked No. 2 for the third straight year. This time, Charlie Pasarell was ahead of me, not Dennis Ralston. I knew I would have to try harder, but weaving a delicate path between my roles as Lieutenant Arthur Ashe, U.S. Army, and Arthur Ashe, tennis player, demanded total commitment at a time when the winds of change were altering the face of the sport forever.

6

Speaking Up

I first played Rod Laver in 1959—at Forest Hills in the first round. I was only sixteen at the time, it was my first time playing the Nationals, and Laver was a star, although not yet a force in the sport. I lost that day, just as I was to lose the next seventeen matches to him before finally beating him in 1974 at the Aetna World Cup in Hartford.

Laver and I had similar approaches. We both had streaky-type games that could catch fire. Laver, a lefty, simply did everything a little better, just as Bjorn Borg is that much better from the baseline than Harold Solomon or Eddie Dibbs, which is why they may never beat Borg.

Laver and I had many interesting matches. Earlier in the summer of 1968, he beat me in the semifinals at Wimbledon and went on to win the title. When Laver wanted something badly enough, his racquet could get as torchy as his sandy red hair. He had every shot and was difficult to pass because he was so quick—quicker than Tom Okker. He also had a very good backhand chip return to my forehand. Laver, Dennis Ralston, and Fred Stolle all could chip their return of serves to my forehand volley, which was my weaker volley; it forced me to pop the ball up. The difference was that Laver hit the ball so well on the rise. He could hop all over the ball, sometimes hitting the damn thing off the half-volley or with a semi-lob. His strength matched my weakness, and he was so fast he could cover up his mistakes. And he was fitter than most people gave him credit for. One of the great tennis "crimes" of the past twenty-five years was that Rocket, as he was called, was kept out of Forest Hills, Wimbledon, and the French Open because he was a pro during the years 1963–67. He would have won at least two more Wimbledons.

There are levels in all sports. A No. 60 player can go out with Tom Watson and Jack Nicklaus and stay even for six holes. But on the seventh hole, Jack and Tom may go 1-up. Then, seven holes later, they go 2-up. After twenty-one holes, maybe they pick up another stroke. When you look at it over four days of tournament, all those strokes add up. That's what separated Laver from the pack. Bjorn Borg did the same thing to John McEnroe in their great 1980 Wimbledon final. They battled for almost four hours, McEnroe won that 18–16 fourth-set tiebreaker, but in the fifth set, Borg lifted the level of his game and won. He loses very few five-set matches.

It took me a long time to understand what I had to do to beat someone like Laver. I couldn't just play my game. I learned by watching how others played him. Roy Emerson was quicker at the net than I was and had a better forehand volley. He also was more patient and played the percentages more. Sometimes that's all you need. It's like gambling houses. They work on a 51–49 split; they don't need any more than that and they clean up in the long run. People think the percentage rate is bigger, but it isn't. It's very, very fine in tennis, too. Someone like Roscoe Tanner doesn't play the percentages enough for the size of his game. So he doesn't win his share of majors.

I found that you can't play the percentages all the time. In March of 1968, I was invited by Reverend Jefferson Rogers to make a speech at his Church of the Holy Redeemer in Washington. Rev. Rogers was an associate of Dr. King's and was politically quite active. He had a speaker's forum at his church every Sunday afternoon. I told him army personnel were not allowed to make political speeches. He said I was copping out. We talked about it several times. Finally, I accepted his invitation, knowing it was against regulations.

Arthur Ashe: OFF THE COURT

Racial confrontations were intense in 1968. Militant blacks were challenging Dr. Martin Luther King's peaceful philosophies; many blacks, including me, were finding it difficult to choose a position. The status quo would not do.

I had never made a political speech before and always resented peer pressure from other blacks. I thought it was counterproductive. What do black athletes, most of whom are not politically inclined, have to offer? What makes Sammy Davis, Jr., an expert on race relations? Why must black entertainers bring up race during their performances? Speak out if you've got something to say, I reasoned, otherwise say nothing. But I was in the spotlight and I talked about black responsibility to the cause of justice. The story was carried in the *Washington Post* the next day and I was called on the carpet by my superiors at West Point. I would be in serious trouble if I spoke publicly again, they warned me. After the rebuff, I felt I had been used by the Reverend Rogers. But I gradually admitted to myself that I had a strange sense of satisfaction for speaking out. I knew there would be trouble if I made the speech, but I accepted rebuke as my way of paying dues to the cause. After all, I had done nothing in the sixties but play tennis and enjoy life. The seventies would be different. Ironically, Reverend Rogers and I now collaborate on many projects.

The speech released a great deal of anxiety and guilt I had repressed and marked the beginning of a period of political activity—in and out of tennis. I became more serious and started to notice political elements I had ignored in certain situations. Later, back at West Point, the new cadets were in "beast barracks," an intensely dehumanizing experience designed to break them down so they could be reconstructed into military men. I was deeply disturbed by the practice and wondered if it was necessary. After eighteen months I concluded it was.

That spring also marked a low point in the war in Vietnam. During one stretch, it seemed there was a funeral every day at West Point. I was saddened to see so many young men, so young they had not even been promoted to first lieutenant, brought back in boxes that reminded us of the consequences of our business. I never thought this war made sense. Seeing the dead and knowing that a disproportionate number of young blacks were paying the ultimate price for faulty American foreign policy, moved me toward firm opposition to our involvement in Southeast Asia, even with my military status.

The week after my speech, I went back to Washington to hear the next guest on the speakers' forum, Stokely Carmichael, who had coined the phrase "black power" in Greenville, Mississippi. After his speech, we had a chance to talk and he gave me two pieces of advice: boycott the Davis Cup because of South Africa's participation and buy a gun.

Several weeks later, while driving across the George Washington Bridge to the city, a bulletin interrupted Richard Harris's "MacArthur Park" on WABC. The announcement: Dr. Martin Luther King had been shot on the balcony of a Memphis hotel. Reports were vague about his fate; I wanted to pull over, but I was in the middle of the bridge. Once I got off, I pulled to a stop on Amsterdam Avenue. A number of black people had done the same thing and were listening to the bulletins. Some got out of their cars and talked about the shooting. Their reactions ranged from sorrow to anger. We all assumed some white man did it.

I can't recall a year that was filled with more drama for me. Each week seemed to bring revelations. In February, the USTA appointed Bob Kelleher as president, an important move in view of Kelleher's progressive thinking. In March, the International Tennis Federation finally approved the principle of open tennis after Wimbledon officials put a gun to its head and said they were going to open the doors to the pros whether the ITF liked it or not. And I'll never forget that day at West Point when I watched President Lyndon Johnson on TV say he would not run again. I was in the Bachelor Officers' Quarters when Johnson said, "I will not run, I shall not accept my party's nomination." April brought the tragedy of Dr. King's death and the first open tournament at Bournemouth where Mark Cox, a British amateur, beat Gonzales.

Our first Davis Cup tie, against the British Caribbean, took place at Byrd Park in Richmond, where I could neck and furtively make love but had been barred a decade earlier from playing tennis. It was a homecoming of sorts because the city made a big deal of my return. I could have held a grudge for all the previous injustices Richmond blacks had suffered, but I began to forgive the city for its past injuries. After all, they were trying to right some of those wrongs. I felt I should meet them more than halfway. Besides, I had an obligation to make things better for those who would follow me. My family still lived there. The West Indies team played well, but we won easily. We were developing team spirit and gaining a reputation under the guidance of our coach Dennis Ralston and Donald Dell.

South Africa was beaten before we had to play them, but it seemed like I was constantly involved in political activity that year. Bobby Kennedy was assassinated in June, an event that shattered all of us, especially Donald. Donald had been as committed to Bobby as he was to regaining the Cup for the United States. He was torn about taking the Cup captaincy because he had been working as an advance man in Bobby's campaign. After our Davis Cup match against Mexico in Berkeley, California, Donald, Charlie, and I went to Sacramento for an exhibition. Bobby had a campaign train that was touring central California. One week later, he was dead.

At Wimbledon, there was considerable talk about a black boycott of the Mexico City Olympics. During a practice session, Donald and I had our first lengthy conversation about life and tennis. Because he was captain, I felt I had to tell him how I felt about the Olympics and South Africa. He was aware of the speech I had made because he lived in Washington and read newspaper accounts. My Southern antennae told me he was OK. Donald liked making decisions and solving problems. He had gone to Landon Prep in Washington and attended Yale on a scholarship. He told me he once overheard his parents talk about how they had skipped much-needed dental work to send their kids through school. Donald was stunned at the time, but it added to his respect for his parents. He went to the University of Virginia Law School, one of the best in the country, and worked for a major law firm until he was recruited by Robert Kennedy and Sargent Shriver.

In years to come, Donald would play an important role in my life as a friend and lawyer. Donald's impatience can get him into trouble sometimes. He is so bright that he believes he can do two or three things at once. Once, he stepped out of a car in London and was crossing the street when an idea came to mind. He took a step, looked left, and was promptly hit by a car coming from the right. His leg was broken, and for a while at least he had to think of just one thing—getting healed.

The only time I have ever seen Donald visibly shaken was when he went to the hospital to have some polyps removed from the lining of his throat. He loved to talk and we noticed his voice was getting increasingly hoarse. We thought the rasp was amusing, but he was petrified when the doctor told him he needed the operation. The doctor also told him he wouldn't be allowed to talk for about a week afterward. That was almost as frightening to Donald as going under the knife. Even his two young twin daughters, Alexandra and Kristina, thought his concern was funny. Alexandra is my goddaughter.

Many black people have told me that I am a fool for

trusting Donald so much. Some white people resent his influence. I suppose trust is one of my weaknesses. I want to believe in the goodness of people. I'm not cynical and I don't think I'm too naive. I know the probable consequences of most of my actions. It's just that it doesn't bother me that much for someone to trick me. I simply stop trusting that person from that point. I had a protected life; for that reason I give everybody the benefit of the doubt and sometimes you pay a price for it. But Donald was more than a friend and business adviser. As a former top-ten player, he understood what was happening on the tennis court. The week before the Open, I was playing Bob Lutz in the finals of the U.S. Amateur championships at Longwood. That year, they had to distinguish between the U.S. Open and the Nationals because they were both major titles. Before the final, Donald reminded me, "You don't want to wake up tomorrow morning having lost this match." I'm sure he must have told Lutz something similar, just as he talked to Clark Graebner and me in the locker room after the third set of our semifinal in the U.S. Open.

The U.S. Open

"Let's end it in four," Donald Dell said, standing in front of my cubicle in the oak-paneled room under the stadium at the West Side Tennis Club.

"Okker looks a little tired," Charlie Pasarell chimed in, trying to lift my spirits.

"I don't see how he can be that tired," I said, staring at Okker, who was seated a few cubicles away. "The games are going too fast."

"You can win it," Clark Graebner whispered. "Just keep the pressure on."

For almost two weeks, I had kept the pressure on opponents in the first U.S. Open championship. Now, leading two sets to one against Tom Okker in the men's singles final, I was one set from the biggest tournament title of my career.

Okker's incentive to win the U.S. Open was strong. As an amateur attached to the United States Army, I was ineligible for prize money, let alone the $14,000 first prize. All I was legally entitled to during the tournament was $28-a-day expenses; because I was a member of the Davis Cup team, the USTA paid for my hotel room. In fact, if we had not beaten Spain at a Davis Cup interzone match in Cleveland, I probably would not have had enough leave time from West Point to spend two weeks at Forest Hills. Okker, however, had "registered" as a professional with his national association; under international rules at the time, he could play for the money. After he beat another pro, Ken Rosewall, in the semifinals and I stopped Clark Graebner, who also was an amateur, in four sets, the USTA was obliged to pay Okker the $14,000 regardless of how he did against me. But Okker wanted a major title.

Gene O'Connor, the Davis Cup trainer, motioned for me to move to a table in a corner of the room. I hopped on, and Gene began massaging my legs.

"What about a shower?" he asked.

"You know I never shower during a match, Gino."

Before tiebreakers became an integral part of the sport, all best-of-five set matches in major championships had ten-minute breaks between the third and fourth sets. Many players used the occasion to shower, change clothes, meditate, or talk tactics with a coach or friend. I never took a shower during the break because I felt I would lose too much heat that way. Evaporation is a cooling process, and I didn't want to cool off. I would rather take a hot towel and rub it over the top part of my body. I had seen too many players cool off, mentally and physically, while leading two sets to one.

"How do you feel?" Donald asked. As the Davis Cup captain, he had watched me in best-of-five set cup victories over the British Caribbean, Mexico, Ecuador, and Spain that year. Today, Davis Cup matches still utilize the ten-minute break because no tiebreakers are used.

"I'm fine," I said.

"Just keep getting your first serve in," Donald preached. "Don't give him any chances to get back in the match."

I had won the first set, 14–12, and felt confident that I could sweep the next two. But true to his nickname, "The Flying Dutchman" hung in and took the second, 7–5, before I won the third, 6–3.

It was a strange final. The match had been postponed from Sunday to Monday because of rain, so the stands, which normally might have been packed on a weekend, were only about half full. Another surprise was the absence of Rod Laver from the final. Everybody had pegged him as the logical men's champion.

Laver was easily the world's No. 1 player. He dominated the sixties the way Borg emerged as the men's star of the seventies. In 1962, Laver won the Grand Slam as an amateur by taking the French, Wimbledon, U.S., and Australian titles. He would do it a second time in 1969, as a pro. If Laver had been my opponent at Forest Hills that day, my whole career might have been different. Laver owned me.

Of course, Laver owned a lot of players. But he seemed to have a special knack for taking my game apart, and my performance at Forest Hills in 1968 may have contributed to his passion for beating me in the future. But Laver never got to the quarters that year; Cliff Drysdale upset him in the round of sixteen.

Drysdale was a South African who later moved to the United States because he was offended by South Africa's apartheid policy. He was one of those players who somehow gave Laver fits over the years. That's one of the ironies of tennis: there are players you know you can beat and others who will frustrate the hell out of you. I always felt confident against Roy Emerson, Laver's Australian countryman, whom I beat in the third round in straight sets. Yet Laver always had trouble with a left-handed Egyptian named Ismail El Shafei, even though El Shafei hardly beat anyone else of note—except me. Dennis Ralston's wide-angled serve and big first volley bothered Laver, and Okker's quickness kept him in rallies with Laver.

Okker won the fourth set, 6–3. After two hours of tennis, we were even. The crowd was drained and silent. I looked up and saw Donald, Charlie, and Clark seated in the stands. Charlie nodded as if to say, "Don't worry, just get on with it."

Fifth sets of tennis matches separate the great from the good. It clearly defines a player's level, just as the difference between a Tom Watson and the sixtieth player on the pro golf tour is about one shot per seven holes.

Physically, I was in the best shape of my life. Being stationed at the United States Military Academy in West

Point had allowed me to beef up that winter, thanks to a weight-training program. The academy's wrestling coach designed a program which enabled me to eventually bench-press 200 pounds. When Lt. Hank Friedman, my roommate, wasn't watching in our Bachelor Officers' Quarters, I would measure my arms and chest. I also ran twenty minutes a day to keep the muscles stretched and drove into New York City four and five nights a week to practice with Gene Scott or Dick Savitt.

The routine improved my stamina and strength. Playing Davis Cup kept me competitively tough, and the restrictions of military life focused my political views in a positive way.

When I started the fifth set against Okker, I was riding a crest of confidence from a string of twenty-four straight singles victories that summer. If I just hold my serve, I told myself, I'll win. I wasn't thinking, I was playing.

I went back to serve the first game of the final set, and everything seemed to be building. My father was in the stands. So was Dr. Johnson. It was the first U.S. Open. As long as the game would be played, whether at the West Side Tennis Club or the National Tennis Center, there would be only one "first" U.S. Open. The events of that year had prepared me for the pressures of the moment.

Against Okker, I had served fifteen aces in the first set. But Okker would run around his backhand on my second serve and hammer his forehand cross-court into my forehand volley. Between the third and fourth sets, Donald kept harping, "Get your first serve in, don't miss your first volley." Seeing him in the stands on the changeover after the first game of the fifth set, brought back the basics again: first serve in, make the first volley, don't miss any returns on your opponent's serve in the first two games. Simple, though not as easy as it sounds.

I held serve for 1–0. I took my position to receive serve, with Dick Savitt's words from the stands also still ringing in my ears. "Christ, bend your knees, kid. For Christ sake, bend your knees," Savitt would shout, a cry that became familiar over the years. He was a former Wimbledon champion himself.

I tried crouching and deep knee bends before Okker served, to remind myself to stay low. Bending knees had never been one of my strong points. It wasn't a matter of laziness. My style had matured on hard courts, where the ball bounces consistently high. At six feet one inch, I never felt as comfortable crouching to return serve as someone like Laver did. But you have to adopt a clinical approach when times get tight. When you get nervous and wonder about winning or losing, you go back to the basics: make the other player miss before you do. Don't give away the easy points with unforced errors. That statement will elicit a chuckle from quite a few of my contemporaries.

With Okker serving at 30-all, I floated a lob inside the baseline. Suddenly, I was at break point. An angled forehand gave me the game. I felt confident. If I could hold serve the rest of the way, the match was mine.

At 4–2, I lost the flow on my serve. Okker leaped on a second spin serve at 30-all and passed me with one of his pet looping forehands. One more point and the match would be back on serve. I could hardly afford to give Okker any more chances.

Okker has one of the game's better attacking forehands. But his backhand has never been a weapon. At 30–40, I decided to make him hit backhand returns even if it meant slowing the pace on my serves. I faulted my first serve, but Okker drove a backhand return wide on my second serve. Deuce. Another first-serve fault. Again, I kept my second serve deep to his backhand; he returned long. I held serve for 5–2 with another second serve to the backhand that he pushed into the net.

Okker would not quit. He held serve. 5–3. Now I had to serve out the match. It was in my hands.

I went for the ace and got it. The momentum was there.

111

I held at love as Okker waved his racquet helplessly at my last forehand volley.

After two hours and forty minutes, I could hardly believe it was over. I spun, stood at crouched attention like a well-drilled West Point cadet and aimed my racquet handle at the tarpaulin-covered stadium wall. I walked slowly behind the umpire's chair, clasped my hands, and then held them up as if a fifteen-round decision had just been announced in my favor.

The award ceremony that day will always hold a special place in my heart. My father came onto the court with me, and it felt wonderful to share that moment with him. Dr. J. was in the stands. Bob Kelleher introduced me as "General Ashe," as I laughed and hugged my father. He was crying.

My father is an emotional man. He cries quite easily over things that touch him, and it's nothing that he's ashamed of. He feels comfortable with it, but I hadn't seen him cry like that in years. When he said, "Well done, son," I knew how much that moment must have meant to him. I was at a loss for words—I mean at a time like that you don't have to say anything—so I put my arm around him because I wanted him to share it with me. It was special. After what he had been through, there are moments you want to share with somebody who is close to you and with no one else. And the public was aware of the social significance of my victories at Longwood and Forest Hills.

On the same day I had won at Longwood, three country clubs in the Washington, D.C., area had dropped out of a women's tennis league because another club had a black player. The player happened to be the wife of Carl T. Rowan, former director of the United States Information Agency and the American ambassador to Finland. *The New York Times* even went so far as to comment editorially on the situation and the reasons blacks had become so impatient. "It is 11 years since Althea Gibson won at Wimbledon and Forest Hills," *The Times* wrote. "But it is shockingly obvious that those who run many American country clubs do not yet know the score."

I knew the score. But this was only the first U.S. Open, and many people were uncertain what would happen afterward. Would open tennis fall flat on its face? Some traditionalists in the USTA would have enjoyed seeing open tennis fail. But if the sport was going to make it in a country that could afford to bankroll the open game, it was important that an American player win the first U.S. Open, just as Chrissie Evert came along at the perfect time after Billie Jean King to boost women's tennis. Then, two years after Chrissie made her debut in 1971, Jimmy Connors marched on the scene. Timing.

Being thrust on center stage gave me a great opportunity to reach people. The week after I won the Open, I appeared on *Face the Nation,* the first athlete ever invited on the show. I talked about the role of the black athlete in professional sports and how it related to the momentum that was building as a result of civil rights legislation. The black community obviously expected overnight victories once LBJ put his signature on that piece of paper. It didn't happen like that, and there was a great deal of frustration among blacks.

The disproportionate share of black GIs in Vietnam created further tensions about unfulfilled promises and expectations. For about five years, a feeling of entitlement existed in the black community. We were entitled to the best; if we didn't get it, we rioted. In professional sports, the momentum didn't gather until the seventies. Wilt Chamberlain broke new ground in the sixties with his $100,000 pro basketball contract, but the big money in pro sports was still around the corner.

I was shocked when an account executive from Dean Witter called and said that an anonymous woman donor had given me one hundred shares of General Motors stock after the U.S. Open. I tried to find out who the person was, but the executive told me, "I'm instructed not to tell you." At the time, the stock sold for about eighty-four dollars a share.

I was even more speechless on my return to West Point. I was invited to dinner in the Great Hall with the cadets. I'll never forget the 3½-minute standing ovation they gave me. Only a few people have been so honored by the entire corps at mess. I knew how special this outpouring was, and I was grateful.

My official duties at the data-processing center kept me busy during my stay at West Point. But my desire to win the Davis Cup took an even greater hold later that fall after we beat India in Puerto Rico and qualified for the finals against Australia in Adelaide. I also developed a minor case of "tennis elbow."

I had been a Davis Cup fan all my life. I had read all the results, remembered the 1955 U.S.-Australia match in Sydney when Tony Trabert and Vic Seixas played against Ken Rosewall and Lew Hoad and drew twenty-five thousand spectators. I was so close to having my name etched on that huge silver bowl. It is hard now to describe the excitement we felt when we realized we were just one series from recapturing a cup that had been out of American possession for five years. Players today are more money-oriented, which is natural since so much more money is involved. Nippon Electronic Corporation, the Davis Cup sponsor in 1981, will spend $1 million on the competition. The winning team gets to split $200,000. In 1955, all the finalists got for their efforts were newspaper headlines.

On paper, we were favored to beat the Aussies. Their best players had turned pro and were ineligible. We had lost only two matches in competition and I was the U.S. Open champion. Clark won his match against Bill Bowery to give us a 1–0 lead. I had to play Ray Ruffels, who was

114

on a winning streak at the time. Ruffels was left-handed. I was soon down a set and a break. During the ten-minute rest period after the third set, Dennis Ralston told me to move over to my left to stop him from swinging his lefty serve so wide.

"You're too tentative," Donald said. "That's not your game. Hit out more when you have an opening."

Donald's advice paralleled what Harry Hopman had told Fred Stolle four years earlier when Stolle was down 3–1 in the fifth set to Ralston in Cleveland. I did the same thing. I moved to my left to return serve and went for the lines whenever I had an opening. I won in four sets, and we were up 2–0 in our quest. Five years earlier, Ralston had helped win the cup on the very same court.

That Thursday night the team, my father, and Bob Kelleher had dinner together. Bob flew down to the scene of his original triumph five years earlier. On Friday morning, I couldn't stand to watch the doubles match. I was too nervous. Graebner and I rode around Adelaide in our team car, turning the radio on and off following the fortunes of Stan Smith and Bob Lutz as they tried to finish it off. The reality of winning was beginning to sink in. I thought of sitting in the dollar seats as a twelve-year-old in Richmond, watching the Aussies play. I was so close to getting my name on that old bowl. Now, in an automobile, on the other side of the world, too anxious to be in the tennis stadium with seven thousand tennis-mad Australians and a handful of Americans, I heard the winning point over the radio. The dream had come true. All the hours and days of travel, practice, strange hotel rooms, foreign accents, aching shins and elbows had converged on this point in time. It was worth it. We had won the Davis Cup.

Beyond the Davis Cup victory was a future we could not see clearly. In its broad outlines, it promised a living from what we loved to do—play tennis. But there was still a great deal to be resolved and as factions battled, national and international tennis bureaucracies jockeyed for position, and tennis players sorted through the competing claims, positions, offers, and threats in search of the ideal situation. And seated in the stands unbeknownst to us was one Carole Osche, a stewardess for Pan Am. She flew over to watch us in Adelaide because she loved tennis. Three years later she would become Mrs. Donald Dell.

After we left Australia, we came back through Southeast Asia: Vietnam, Burma, Laos, Cambodia, Indonesia, Thailand, Hong Kong, the Philippines, and Japan. We were playing tennis for the troops and visiting hospitals and military installations. In Saigon, we had lunch with Ambassador Ellsworth Bunker at his home. He was the subject of numerous newspaper articles because of the controversy about the course of the war. But his manner at his home there was more like that of a businessman who had just shot 80 on the golf course. Bunker was a very optimistic gray-haired gentleman. He lived just across the back alley from the "best little whorehouse in Saigon." Two days later, some of us went to visit the place so highly recommended. We found it terribly amusing to tell each other that "a couple of days ago we had lunch across the alley at the finest little embassy in Saigon."

General Creighton Abrams gave us a personal briefing on the progress of the war. Inside his MAC-V Headquarters, he described the Corps areas and pointed them out on a map. He talked in the language of that war. Abrams explained that sweeps were conducted by putting a lot of men into an area you suspected of harboring the enemy. The soldiers moved through that area and if they encountered any Vietcong they dealt with them. I was reminded of the way we used to hunt deer in Virginia. One man, usually a friend of my father's, Mr. Sutton, would take the dogs around behind the area where we thought the deer was hiding and work his way toward the rest of us while we waited in the semicircle.

116

Another feature of the war was the search-and-destroy mission. Patrols were sent out. If they ran into the enemy, they radioed in and reinforcements were flown in by helicopter. It sounded very cut and dry.

General Abrams was very patient with his explanations, but I wasn't sold. The fact that I was an army officer traveling in civilian clothes didn't prevent me from telling him I thought the whole thing was ridiculous.

"Well, we're trying to contain communism here. If we don't, you'll wind up fighting them on our shores. Take your pick," the general said. My brother was in the Marines and had recently told me he would be coming over to Vietnam. I was upset, even though some strange instinct told me he would be all right there.

"Morale is my biggest problem, even among the officers," the general told us.

I asked him about black soldiers. He talked about the serious drug problem and the easy availability of heroin, marijuana, cocaine, mescaline, and virtually every conceivable drug. Blacks were among the serious drug users, but they were hardly the only ones, Abrams said.

"Soon, I'll have a brother over here," I told the general.

"Hopefully, we'll finish by then," he said. Of course, he was wrong.

We went to the hospital at Longbinh. It was across the street from the Longbinh Jail, popularly known as The LBJ. We played an exhibition on the hospital grounds. In the middle of a doubles match between Pasarell and me against Smith and Lutz, several rounds of mortar fell some miles away. We could see the puffs of smoke followed by the tell-tale crump. We became quite nervous and at one point Lutz dropped his racquet and started to run off the court. The soldiers in the bleachers were amused and watched the mortar rounds without moving. We were embarrassed, but we had not gone through the initiation to real war.

This was our first contact with the consequences of the

117

war. There were men in the hospital with syphilis and malaria, and also men with very serious injuries. We were stunned by what we saw. For the first time, the full impact of the war was brought home. We saw GIs who had lost their eyes, part of a face, arms, or legs. We saw jaws wired shut or eyes closed and greased to keep the lids from fusing shut.

It was difficult to absorb, especially so for Lutz. Until that time, Bob had been happy-go-lucky, but the experiences in Vietnam had a visible effect on him. At one point, he was talking to a guy in a body cast. The man started to cough. A nurse came over and gently pushed Bob along, assuring him she'd take care of the patient. Some time later, we learned the man had died.

I view my escape from the war as one of the great omissions of my life. It may sound barbaric and inhumane but I've always wanted to be in a war. Perhaps it is a death wish of sorts. I think every man wishes secretly that he would have an opportunity to fight, win lots of medals, and come out only with minor injuries. War is the ultimate symbol of Western masculinity. Unfortunately.

My tour of Southeast Asia and Japan confirmed the universal nature of the color problem. The racism of Asia was a fascinating counterpoint to that of America and the British Commonwealth. The Japanese and the Mandarin Chinese of Hong Kong felt they were a cut above other Orientals. In Manila, a shopkeeper said of Japanese visitors, "Yes, they look down on us. They come over here to our girlie houses. In fact, the Japanese are our biggest customers, but they don't like us."

My anthropology professor at UCLA hadn't told me there were two types of Orientals: yellow and brown. The Japanese and Chinese sat at the top of the pecking order, with the Burmese, Laotians, Cambodians, and Vietnamese at the bottom and the Koreans and Thais somewhere in the middle. I had heard my brother use the term "gooks" but had to make a real effort to believe they were all that bad. It was a sentiment shared by many black GIs I met in Vietnam. "I ain't got no quarrel with them Vietcong," said Muhammad Ali, and many soldiers had great sympathy with Vietnamese villagers. "On that last sweep," a GI told me, "I saw some scenes that reminded me of home in Marion, Alabama. I sure didn't want to shoot nobody but they all walk around in them black PJs and they all look alike." He chuckled. "This is a bad war."

When I was in the juniors, there was a dark-skinned Filipino on the tour named Willie Hernandez. Like Jean Baker, he was often mistaken for a fair-skinned black American and he didn't like it at all. It wasn't so much that he was being associated with blacks but that he felt Filipino.

In Hong Kong, the rickshaw drivers were not likely to be Chinese at all. This was also true of the baggage handlers at the Hong Kong airport. I was beginning to believe that the entire world was stratified by skin color. I once saw two white skycaps at Los Angeles airport. It was so striking I went up to one and asked, "Forgive me for being so presumptuous. I've never seen a white skycap before. How did you get your job?"

He opened his mouth to answer. As soon as I heard the Spanish accent, I said to myself, "That explains it." But he went on to say how he had seen the airport personnel director and was hired. I told him I was a veteran traveler and had come to believe that the brothers had these jobs locked up. He didn't understand but told me he had never been on an airplane. He couldn't have known about black skycaps because he never traveled by air.

You might wonder about my fascination with the issue of color. It is something related to my past and something I saw wherever I went. I had to catalogue the phenomenon and make some sense of it for my own value system. South African apartheid aside, there are many explana-

Arthur Ashe: OFF THE COURT

tions about the dominance of light-skinned people in certain jobs and positions of power. I worry about the possible effect of this phenomenon on children who grow up and believe their chances in life are not going to be as good because of their skin color.

My travels convinced me of the importance of role models. But young black children especially need to become accustomed to seeing someone black in a position of authority and to believe that such opportunities are open to them. It may be even more important for young whites, because twenty years from now they may be in a position to make a difference. If their cultural and racial values are not put on the right track there will be serious obstacles to real progress in relationships between the various races in this country and elsewhere.

My tour of Vietnam was interrupted so I could fly to Syracuse, New York. The Jaycees had selected me for one of their Ten Outstanding Young Men award. I found it ironic that I had been picked in 1968 when eight years earlier I couldn't play in their tournaments. I had decided at some point not to become bitter about the past, but I made a strong speech at the ceremony.

Because of the Davis Cup win we got to meet President Johnson. I recalled his "I am not going to run for president" speech during my stay at West Point and was impressed by his style. He had a firm handshake and chatted with us for a few minutes. During our visit, Lynda Bird Johnson asked about my father. She had seen him cry at the end of the U.S. Open earlier that summer and wanted to know more about him.

The man we really got to know better was Vice President Hubert Humphrey. Charlie and I went to his office, and he spent a fair amount of time with us. He was a voluble, open person who was instantly likable. I think he could have been a tough and stern president when the situation called for it but he didn't become president because he

120

didn't project that capability to the people. He had the knack of making you feel he had nothing else to do and that you were very special to him.

"When you were in the Senate," I asked, "did you vote the way your constituents would want you to, or did you use your best judgment?"

"It was a little of both," he told us. He explained that he represented the people of Minnesota so he had to bring their view of issues to Congress. However, most people tend to be parochial, and sometimes you have to do what you think is best for all the people even if Minnesotans don't benefit greatly from a particular decision.

I gave a lot of thought to politics in those days and was even thinking that someday I might run for political office. I admired Humphrey and my respect for him grew when I saw how he kept his strength and dignity to the end of his life. How people die is important, especially when they're public figures. John Wayne died well, literally with his boots on. I knew he was a nice old right-winger, but I had tears in my eyes when I saw him at the Academy Awards just before his death.

It was a very emotional time for me. We had won the Davis Cup. The memory of the Mexico City Olympics and the black-gloved demonstration by Tommie Smith and John Carlos, the two black American sprinters, was still fresh in my mind. I spoke out more and got positive feedback from blacks and whites, even with my military status.

At one time, blacks saw the Armed Forces as a way of pressing their demands for equality. People my father's age saw more opportunity inside the military than in civilian life. During World War I, black leaders had seen the war as an opportunity to press our case for fair treatment by fighting alongside whites. But that effort had failed. Black soldiers coming home from Europe were harassed, beaten, and killed while still in uniform by whites who feared they had become too uppity after consorting with white women and killing white German men. The race riots of 1919 were worse than those in the 60s.

Dr. King's public opposition to the Vietnam War was a courageous position to take in 1966. But in the 1980s, it has become commonplace for black leaders to oppose large arms expenditures because they equate large defense budgets with cutbacks in social programs. After the briefing with General Abrams and the admission later that the only way to stop the North Vietnamese was to bomb the hell out of them—something Nixon eventually did at the urging of Henry Kissinger—I could only conclude the war was absurd and meaningless.

During my stint at West Point, I made friends with Scott Day, the son of the registrar at the Academy. Scott had had mental problems all his life. He just couldn't cope with life. Somehow he took a liking to me and often wrote to me. He moved to Miami, drove a cab, and wrote me four or five long letters a year to explain what was going through his head and the difficulties he was having.

His father left the Academy and became director of the Tennis Hall of Fame in Newport, Rhode Island, so I saw Colonel Day fairly often after I left West Point. One day he told me Scott had committed suicide. The shock was devastating, although in a way we had expected it. Not long before, I had received a letter from Scott telling me he was glad I had been his friend, that he appreciated the letters I had written, and that I would be one of the few people who would understand why he had to do what he was doing.

Another benefit of my status as a tennis player was my access to some interesting people. After a tour of France with the Davis Cup team, I spent Thanksgiving of 1968 in Paris at the U.S. Embassy home of Sargent Shriver, the American ambassador to France. Hubert Humphrey had lost the election to Richard Nixon and the Shrivers would soon be moving back to the United States. Rose Kennedy was visiting her daughter Eunice; I was impressed by her awareness and mental agility. She was sprightly, outgoing, and talked about her family's origin in Ireland and the best and worst of human civilization. As far as I was concerned, my formal schooling was complete. I was an educated adult, ready to venture into a world that promised a great deal of pleasure, excitement, and challenge.

On the Road

It doesn't surprise me that no more black tennis players have emerged in recent years. Tennis is not an integral part of black lifestyles; until that happens, we are forcing the issue—really forcing it. When will it happen? Not for a while, because the facilities, competition, and coaching are not freely available in the black community. If a black kid today wants to become a tennis player, in effect he has to leave the black community. He can't do it there. And not that many black kids are confident enough and self-disciplined enough to survive in a white world at an early age. I survived because I had somebody holding my hand. I didn't do it myself. Dr. Johnson was one of a kind. The black community has not seen anyone like him since. In fact, there aren't too many people like him in the white community either.

I have often been asked if there are racial differences in athletic ability. I haven't studied the situation systematically, but I can believe there are significant anatomical and cultural differences among the races that would make one group physically superior to another in certain sports. Questions about why the NBA is 70 percent black, why the great running backs in football are black, and why the top heavyweight boxers are black are legitimate. But these inquiries should be pursued with caution because of their implications. There is an assumption that if blacks are found to be physically superior, they must be intellectually inferior. I ran into that thinking at Stellenbosch University in South Africa. Such inquiries can be dangerous: the professor and his students were using them to justify apartheid.

For the sake of publicizing a good fight, Americans will

categorize opponents to make the battle more attractive commercially. Gerry Cooney is the "Great White Hope" in heavyweight boxing now. Leslie Allen is the "Great Black Hope" in women's tennis. It's natural to categorize people so that you can put one group of followers against another.

It's not a form of racism, but it can be used racially for convenience. There's not a big jump from the time when Southerners who wanted to justify slavery felt that black people had smaller craniums, and thus smaller brains, couldn't think as well, and were suited only to be tillers of the soil, a notion that even Thomas Jefferson thought about.

The suggestion that the large number of blacks on NBA teams has contributed to poor television ratings is a sensitive subject. I think part of the NBA's problem may involve blacks, but not as much as some of the members of the media are claiming.

Race has a hell of a lot to do with the commercial success of sports. A ton. In boxing, Gerry Cooney is worth more because he's white than if he were nonwhite. Leslie Allen's market value is heightened because she is black. It's simple: she sticks out. I stuck out. Althea Gibson stuck out. Gerry Cooney sticks out.

Some blacks resent this phenomenon. Racially, blacks are paid less than whites at certain positions in pro football, with the exception of running backs. But in basketball, the highest paid players are black. If a white basketball player came by and said, "Jesus, I think they're discriminating against whites because certain whites don't make as much as certain blacks," the black community would say, "Don't hand us that. First of all, it's not true; secondly, we deserve it anyway for a while." But we blacks must be consistent with our complaints without crying wolf too often needlessly.

Stereotypes are perpetuated in jokes, like the notion

125

that "blacks are good dancers because they have good rhythm." Everybody laughs, but many a truth is spoken in jest. Secretly, blacks may be proud of being good dancers and ballplayers. It doesn't make us any less proud of an O. J. Simpson, Walter Payton, or Kareem Abdul-Jabbar when they perform well, even though white society may say "all of you are like that." We resent white society lumping us into one pile; we resent the generalization but are proud of the individual.

If I were white—and it's impossible to imagine that except for hypothetical purposes—I believe that if I saw Rick Barry score forty-five points I wouldn't say "I'm proud to be white because Rick Barry scored forty-five points." I would have to narrow it down; for example, if Ernie DeGregorio scored forty-five points, I could say, "I'm proud to be Italian because Ernie D scored forty-five points."

These differences, whether religious or racial, are heavy factors in the success of commercial sports. The people who promote these events want to keep these divisions sharp and clean. They can make more money this way, even with the notion that sports is supposed to be the great equalizer.

In some respects, sports has been an equalizer. I don't believe our society would have gotten as far without the integration of high school, college, and professional sports teams. It doesn't mean that blacks and whites won't notice five white starters on the Brigham Young University basketball teams. I watched the 1981 NCAA playoffs and laughingly told a white friend, "There's the best white team in America." There may still be resentment about ten blacks being on the basketball court at the same time, but to coin that old Virginia Slims phrase, "we've come a long way, baby," and sports has been out in front on this issue.

In tennis, lateral quickness is more important than

color. A tennis ball dropped from the height of the net takes about two seconds to fall, bounce, fall again, and hit the ground a second time. A good player should be able to cover thirty-six feet from the baseline to the net in less than two seconds. Frank Sedgeman, Ken Rosewall, Vitas Gerulaitis, John McEnroe, Johan Kriek, Bjorn Borg, and Rod Laver are the quickest players I have seen. They could all get to that ball before it bounces twice.

Foot-and-eye coordination is more important in tennis than hand-eye coordination. After a long layoff from tennis, my feet got tangled up. The hands and arms don't forget how to swing the racquet, but the feet were another problem. Anybody can swing a racquet. It's the great feet that win Grand Slam titles.

I started on asphalt courts at Brook Field. I developed great ground strokes to get the ball over the net as an eight-year-old. I didn't learn how to volley until St. Louis; as a result my forehand volley was never delicate. I was stiff-armed, and my follow-through on the volley was much too long. At UCLA, J. D. Morgan tried to shorten the follow-through on my forehand volley and help me overcome my deep-seated fear of my forehand. I knew I had a great backhand, but in my transition from clay to hard courts I changed my grip.

Tennis lore says every great player has at least two great shots. My serve was among the best, especially wide to the forehand. Very few right-handed players could swing their serve as wide to the forehand. It pulled my opponent off the court and weakened his return. I felt my backhand was second to none. I was not a great athlete, but I was fast, had quick hands, good hand-eye coordination, and repertoire and attitude came together at a time when the pro game was mushrooming with prize money and commercial endorsements.

I entered the endorsement market in 1969. It was a significant step. A star athlete could expect to make more money off the field than on—if he or she was packaged properly. By "packaging," I don't mean a phony personality, although there have been such instances. But to make money, an athlete does, in essence, sell himself. I had to sell a product—me—and the product had to be of high quality to get a high price. The yardstick, then and now, was Arnold Palmer. He is considered the most successful pro athlete off the field; Palmer has reportedly made $70 million since he turned professional—and most golfers like to say he's still got it all! If my heroes on the field were Jackie Robinson and Willie Mays, I wanted to emulate Arnold Palmer off the court.

Neither Donald Dell nor I knew what being black would do to my chances in the endorsement arena. We had some definite objectives—financial security and a good public image. Very few black athletes had benefited from the off-field cash that was available for white athletes. We decided to assume that blackness was an advantage because I was the only black star on the tennis circuit. I had a good image—U.S. Army, Davis Cup, acceptable manners. My experience indicated I was acceptable to white Americans, who bought the racquets, shoes, and tennis clothes I hoped to sell.

I had always wanted my name on a racquet like Pancho Gonzales, Don Budge, and other tennis players. I had used a Wilson Don Budge since I was thirteen. The model was renamed several times for more current players—a Tony Trabert, Barry MacKay, Alex Olmedo. I felt a loyalty to Wilson. Donald and I sat down with Gene Buwick of Wilson in the Polo Lounge of the Beverly Hills Hotel one day about the possibilities. Wilson was the biggest sporting goods manufacturer in the U.S.; the best years of pro tennis were ahead of us.

What was enough? What was I worth? I had won the U.S. Open, the Davis Cup. I was well known. I had been on the cover of *Life, Sports Illustrated,* and been profiled by the *New Yorker.* I deserved a good price—six figures—because I was black, good, had an admirable reputation, and was American. Being black was a bonus almost. But being American was the most important factor. If Bjorn Borg were American, he could double his off-court income, although he already does well into the millions anyway.

After some protracted negotiations, Donald and I decided Wilson was not willing to pay what we thought I was worth. We were disappointed but tried other pastures. We finally signed a multiyear contract with Head; I would "license" Head to manufacture racquets under my name and endorsement. In return, I would help them promote the racquet and the company. Head and Catalina both informed me that a few of their retailers canceled their orders when I began to endorse the product. It was encouraging to know that both companies said "to hell with them." My being black has not been a problem since.

One of the rules of the wonderful world of tennis endorsements is "if your name is on the product, you are entitled to royalty." The truth is that players who had endorsed racquets as far back as Don Budge had no input into the manufacturing and design of the equipment that carried their names. A breakthrough was made by Lacoste in France. They had made a strange steel racquet that Wilson bought and introduced in the United States as the T-2000. Jimmy Connors seemed to be the only pro who could play with it, but the scramble was on. Terms like "trampoline effect" and "torsional rigidity" suddenly entered the tennis vocabulary.

John Howe, one of Head's engineers, came up with a racquet shaped like an upside-down teardrop with a twin-shafted throat and a three-piece sandwich of aluminum and fiberglass. It was funny looking indeed.

"This is what we want you to play-test," said Joe Boggia, chief of product development for Head at the time.

"You've got to be kidding," I said as I picked it up and swung it a few times. It felt bulky and heavy. "Do you make this in my size—4⅝ medium?"

"We can," he assured me, "but first we want to know how it plays." My role as a consultant had begun. I would have an opportunity to help develop a racquet from scratch.

In 1968, the USTA licensed Catalina to market a line of color-coordinated tennis clothes with the USTA logo. The arrangement didn't last very long. During a 1969 U.S. Open tennis match, Bill Talbert, the director, ordered me to take off my yellow Catalina shirt before I could play.

"This is an official USTA-endorsed piece of tennis clothing," I told Billy.

"I know," he answered. "I'm sorry, but you can't wear it and play in this tournament. You must wear white."

It wasn't Billy's fault. He was just laying down the current law against nonwhite clothes. Alex Lawler, the president of Catalina, was so upset that he cut his ties with the USTA and took me on as his endorser. I had a few tense moments with the association over this issue, but liked wearing colorful clothes and the rule was eventually changed. Now, anything goes.

My economic position took shape in unusual ways. One day, Ike Bomzer, the doorman at the Tuscany Hotel in New York, overheard the owners of the Tuscany, Howard Kaskel and Al Schragis, talking about improving the tennis facilities at their Doral Country Club in Miami. I had learned long ago that doormen all over the world are important people because they know everything and will do anything for you if you treat them properly; Ike was a friend.

"I know the perfect guy for you," Ike told his bosses, recommending me. Mr. Kaskel and Mr. Schragis were interested. I flew to Miami; and they were willing to take a chance. So was Joe Cullman, the chairman of the board at

Philip Morris, who started a management training program for Rafael Osuna, Roy Emerson, Manuel Santana, and me. All of us were past winners at Forest Hills—Rafe in 1963, Roy in 1961 and 1964, Santana in 1965, and me in 1968, and Joe envisioned us contributing as Philip Morris executives in our various countries.

Both Doral and Philip Morris have been rewarding. I have been the Tennis Director at Doral for eleven years. They took a chance with a black pro at an overwhelmingly white club, but it worked.

At Philip Morris, I did not work for the cigarette division for obvious reasons. On promotional trips for them around the world I got to meet such people as Alexander Haig and General David Jones, who is now chairman of the Joint Chiefs of Staff. Some conversations proved to be real eye-openers.

One primary promotional activity in 1971 was the personal appearance. I did "store appearances" for Catalina, Philip Morris, and Head and tennis clinics for American Airlines and All-American Sports, a tennis camp headed at one time by Nick Bollettieri. A store appearance meant autographing pictures and answering questions for from one to four hours. Sometimes, I did two appearances in the same day. Many athletes dislike the store appearance, but I understood that customers bought my clothes and racquets. One of the first things I did was to throw out the staid approach of my fellow athletes and inject a little theater into the appearances. I would get customers involved by using them in demonstrations. I would turn the tables and ask the audience questions. The appearance definitely solidifies the relationship between the manufacturer, store, and customer. The store gets the athlete for either a very low fee or guarantees the manufacturer a minimum order. What I disliked was the tendency of some fans to get personal. Some women asked for a kiss on the cheek instead of a photograph, and once in a while someone would slip me a piece of paper with a telephone number on it.

Life on the pro circuit is a combination of "what's next?" and "can you believe this?" At times airports and cities are a blur, and I share Guillermo Vilas's notion that tennis players think more by weeks than days.

A good example was my trip to West Africa in 1971 with Charlie Pasarell, Tom Okker, and Marty Riessen. Charlie was married to Shireen Fareed the day before we left for Africa. The wedding was in Los Angeles on a Saturday night, then we caught the "red-eye" night flight to New York, where I paid for his wedding night at the Doral-on-the-Park, the sister hotel of the Doral Country Club in Miami, where I am the Tennis Director. On Sunday night, he, his bride, and I were off to Dakar.

We spent three weeks in Senegal, Cameroon, Gabon, and the Ivory Coast. In Yaunde, Cameroon, we were driving into the grounds of a tennis club one day when we saw a little brown-skinned kid hitting on one of the courts. He was whacking the ball very well, and we were quite impressed. I found out his mother was French and his father African. His name was Yannick Noah.

Later, I got on the telephone to Philippe Chatrier, the President of the French Tennis Federation. "One of your 'colonials' down here plays pretty well," I said jokingly.

"How old is he?" Philippe asked.

"I'd say about eleven."

"You say he's good?"

"Excellent, but he's not going to go very far if he doesn't get out of the Cameroons. I'll pay his way to France for you to take a look at him." Nine years later, Yannick Noah was the No. 1 player in France.

Over the years, my connection with Yannick has been overpublicized. People wanted a Hollywood-type script, particularly when he won a tournament in my home town,

Richmond, in 1981. Yes, I saw him in 1971, I knew he had a lot of talent and I phoned Philippe. I called attention to him, but it was Philippe, in his desire to restore French tennis to the grandeur of the Four Musketeers of the 1920s, who made it happen, along with his coaches, Patrice Benst, Jean-Paul Lath, and Patrice Hagelaner. One of his biggest dreams has been for France to win the Davis Cup; he would be in tears if that happened, and Noah can help him achieve that joy.

Yannick Noah is not my protégé. I didn't teach him a single stroke. We played doubles together at Wimbledon, and I arranged practice courts for him one year at Eastbourne, before Wimbledon. But Yannick and I are not that close. I see him, I say hello, and maybe we'll have a five-minute conversation here and there. But that's it. I'm sure people would like to believe that Yannick and I, because we're black and I supposedly "discovered" him, are tight. There was a lot of resentment over this issue among some black American players on the circuit. Of course, they only knew what they read in the paper, and no one bothered to ask me. I found out about the resentment through the grapevine in 1980 and it turned out to be true.

People expect things from me which they have no right to expect. Their rationale was, "Well, Arthur's a brother and he should be helping us out more than he's helping Yannick Noah." What they didn't realize was that I wasn't helping Yannick that much.

I'll be glad to give anyone advice. I've helped Rodney Harmon and Chip Hooper. Both are promising black American players; Rodney also is from my hometown, and I know how much it meant when some people from Richmond supported me. But the predicament I'm in is that if I don't spread out my assistance, people become upset: I become the bad guy and I can't win.

Arthur Ashe: OFF THE COURT

There were other interesting numbers on the tour—like the money that changed hands in our hotels and locker rooms. Once there was a poker game to end all poker games—at least for me. We were holed up in Raul Ramirez's room one day in Teheran playing high-low, low-ball, screw-your-neighbor, and all the other seven-card poker games one could think of. At about 5:30 A.M. after nine hours of playing, there were some heavy winners and heavy losers. The heavy winner was Roger Taylor and the heavy loser was Zeljko Franulovic of Yugoslavia. There was $2,500 in the pot and Roger was declaring high and low—or so Raul thought. Zeljko had A-2-3-4-5; the two and three in his hand and the A-4-5 on the table, face up. Raul had A-3-4-5-6. He thought he had the perfect low hand and was wondering why Zeljko would stay with him, except to go high-low. What Zeljko didn't know was that A-2-3-4-5 is a straight—but high. Roger declared high and won. Raul declared low and won. Zeljko declared both ways and lost. We decided to divide all wins and losses by four to keep it friendly because Zeljko would have lost $1,500. Ray Moore and Hans Kary were also losers that hand.

Another time in Bristol, England, we had a poker game that lasted seventy-two hours—six guys. It had rained for three straight days and there was nothing else to do except play poker. I lost. I'm a terrible poker player.

A typical tour day schedule was like this: get up, eat breakfast, practice, eat or play your match, shower, play doubles, shower again, eat dinner, go to bed. That is the basic routine. It doesn't vary much. I was always amazed at the number of players who seemingly didn't take practice seriously enough. No one can be serious at practice all the time, but I always tried to sneak in at least a good ten minutes of something special—which always turned out to be my forehand volley. After five or six years, the strokes change less and less. Practice then becomes a means of preserving rather than improving a stroke. This was the case with my forehand volley.

I knew how to execute it on paper, but I would freeze a little during play. In 1975, I settled on a different approach. I assumed it would never be a great shot, so I settled for a lesser goal. I would try to make as few errors as possible, which meant not hitting it in the net.

During practice, we made up games to keep from getting bored. There were half-court games, there was "dinkum" that was played completely in the service court on either the left or the right side; you were not allowed to hit the ball hard but could rush the net (from the service line). Tom Leonard was by far the best "dinkum" player of my generation.

During one tour, we were forced to practice on one court because frequently that was all that was available. To enable two separate twosomes to play on one court simultaneously, we invented what we called "Chinese doubles." Two players would play a point and keep score. When the point was over, they would get off the court and two other players would play a point and keep score. After that point, the first twosome would play again.

Sometimes we played "double singles." One team would play another team, but only two could play at once as in singles. Whoever won a point stayed on to play the next point, but the loser made way for his partner.

Then there was "drunken doubles." In this game, which the Aussies loved, "double singles" were played. Instead of playing just points, whole games were played. But the winner of a game had to drink a shot glass full of beer. By the end of an hour, we'd all be "pissed as parrots" as Roy Emerson would say. But it was a lot of fun and nobody cared much who won anyway.

I loved to go into the coffee bars in cities. If you stand at the bar long enough, someone will come up to you and attempt a conversation in broken English. I was always taken to be a soldier, except one girl in Barcelona told me, "I don't think you are soldier because your hairs are too long." When I said "yes," she was right; I also told her that "hair" is O.K. for singular and plural. Thus a conversation was started.

The groupies always found where we were staying and would hang around the bars of our hotels. They invariably spoke at least a little English, as in Germany, France, England, Australia, Sweden. There were seldom any groupies in Italy, Spain, or Japan. Nobody cared in Nigeria. There were no black groupies on the tour that I knew of, and no Orientals.

Quite a few times, some of the pros made it with their hosts, or hostesses. Once in Denver, Ross Case, known as "Snake," was picked up at the airport by his "housing" for the week, as was the case with quite a few tournaments. While most of us were picked up by couples, "Snake" was picked up by a lone woman. On the way home, she told him that she only had "one bedroom and I hope you don't mind sleeping in the same room." Ross was properly shocked, but played it cool until he got to her apartment. Then he found out that she not only had but one bedroom, she only had one bed. "Snake" then proceeded to turn his best performance of the tour—on the court. He got to the semifinals of the singles and doubles.

Backgammon became an absolute passion for a while. As in poker, running tallies were kept over a season and players usually agreed to square all accounts at either Wimbledon or the U.S. Open.

One of the toughest assignments for me was getting a haircut. It was particularly a problem in Australia. Aboriginals all have straight hair and the closest thing to me was a Fijian, whom the Aussies would call a "woolly." Several times I had to try to explain to an Australian barber how to cut my kinky hair. And each time the shaving became "theater." People would literally stop and watch; chances are they would never again see a kinky-haired black man get his hair cut. I know that for a long time several players —especially the Russians—wanted to touch my hair but they never asked. Alex Metreveli, the Russian player, had a coach named Serge. One day, at Albert Hall in London, I came out of the shower, semi-dried my hair, put on my clothes, and then proceeded to "pick" my hair. Serge watched in amazement as my *pick* disappeared into my head and with a flick of my wrist I pulled, teased, and shaped my " 'fro."

"Vat is dat—dust?" he asked.

"No, is not dust. Come here Serge; you can touch it."

He walked over and felt the top of my head while the locker room roared.

"Is soft, not hard. I think long time is hard. Feels nice."

"What does it feel like, Serge?"

He broke out into a big grin and walked out, amid howls of laughter.

Sometimes, time and place seemed to stand still. When my grandmother died in 1972, my Aunt Marie Cunningham reached me in London with the news that "Big Mama" was gone. I caught a plane to Richmond and was plunged into the warm, familiar world of my childhood again: the minister, sweating and singing and preaching, and the choir. I tried to keep my reserve through the service and almost did. But when my Uncle Rudy cried out, "Good-bye, Mama," I broke down and emotions poured out of me, totally out of control. I cried like a baby for several minutes. When it was over, I was drained of tensions I didn't even know had been inside. But it was all right, I was among family and old friends. I was "Arthur Junior" again.

The next day, I was back on a plane, back to London and to the politics of confrontation that would lead to assorted threats, Davis Cup bans, and the 1973 ATP mass withdrawal from Wimbledon.

No one laughed at the big numbers being doled out in prize money. I began to develop a reputation as something of a locker-room lawyer after we formed the International Tennis Players Association in 1969. As treasurer, I kept the money for the ITPA for two and a half years until we formed the Association of Tennis Professionals in 1972. I became active because I wanted to be a part of the decision-making machinery. There had been a time when Virginia's poll tax kept many black people from voting. A man could lose his job at the sawmill, the lumberyard, or the hospital if he was caught voting—poll tax or no poll tax. There were times when I wanted to tell off the whole state of Virginia for the wasted talent—black and white— that slipped away because of discrimination.

What infuriated me most was having a white Richmond type come up to me somewhere in the world and say, "I saw you play at Byrd Park when you were a kid." Nobody saw me at Byrd Park, because when I was a kid it was for whites only.

The year before, the ITF and World Championship Tennis had signed a "peace agreement" to coexist. WCT events would be sanctioned by the ITF and incorporated into the Grand Prix concept. The agreement made us players feel we would be trampled upon; if we didn't stick together, the tennis organizations and WCT would roll right over us.

I don't think Lamar Hunt, the owner of WCT, was prepared for our reaction. I had a five-year contract with WCT, but tennis players were not like football players. If one of his Kansas City Chiefs, the NFL team he owned, got too argumentative, he could be quickly replaced by the coach. Tennis players were accustomed to going and coming at will. We felt at first that WCT was not leveling with us. There were announcements about prize money that we never got. The agreement might mean that the ITF and WCT would join forces to keep down the amounts of the prize money. WCT was not a charitable organization, but we didn't want ceilings placed on the growth of our prize money either. Sentiments were high on both sides, and I even once said in an interview Lamar was "dishonest"; it was eventually straightened out, but the pressure brought about the formation of ATP, in a hotel room in Quebec during a WCT event. The nucleus was John Newcombe, Charlie Pasarell, Mark Cox, Cliff Drysdale, Ismael El Shafei, Ray Ruffels, and me. Cliff was selected as our first president. I was the vice president. The stage was set for a showdown. We didn't know when or where, but sooner or later, we'd be tested and if we didn't weather the test, we'd be back to pre-1968 days.

The test came one year later. Early in June, the Yugoslavian Tennis Federation suspended Nikki Pilic, one of our members, on the grounds that he promised to play Davis Cup and reneged. The ITF upheld the suspension.

One of our basic principles was "free determination of events to play in." We couldn't let the Yugoslavs or the ITF get away with that, so the ATP board met to choose a course of action. Meeting almost every night during the week before Wimbledon, we decided that the suspension was unjust and that "we will not play in any event that honors that phony suspension," which was to last thirty days.

The timing of the suspension was the real problem. Wimbledon was only a week away. If we really meant what we said, we would wind up pulling out of Wimbledon. We met in the Westbury and decided we had no choice; the "peace agreement" had made us "contract pros" eligible for Wimbledon once again, but too much was at stake.

We also had a logistical problem. Captain Mike Gibson, the Wimbledon referee, told us since we had entered individually, we had to withdraw individually. Jim McManus and I ran around Queen's Club (the players' hangout before Wimbledon) with a clipboard and collected signatures from as many ATP members as possible. At the same time, we went to court to try to have the suspension lifted. I had never been to court, but if I were on trial for my life, I would much rather take my chances in a British court. I wasn't a participant, but as vice president of the ATP, I was an interested party. I had read about English courts and their bewigged barristers and judges, and it was as impressive as I had been led to believe. After a few days of deliberation, the judge decided that the court had no jurisdiction in the matter. I felt our cause was right, but agreed with the decision. I understood the politics involved. A decision in our favor would have been a slap in the face for Wimbledon; the case shouldn't have come to court in the first place. We had no choice but to withdraw from the tournament. I felt sorriest for Stan Smith, who couldn't defend his title, and for Ken Rosewall, whose time at the top was running out.

The Wimbledon boycott was unpleasant, but there had been other stimulating rewards on the circuit. In 1970, the state department asked Stan Smith and me to do a tour of Africa. We were joined on the trip by Frank Deford of *Sports Illustrated,* Bud Collins of the *Boston Globe,* and Richard Evans, a freelance writer. Stan played the role of my "opponent" very well, although he was No. 1 in the U.S. at the time and I was No. 2.

"If we tour the South in the U.S.," Stan teased as we left for Africa, "I'll play the Great White Hope."

We were treated royally and stayed at the ambassador's residence in each country. A camera crew from the United States Information Service filmed the trip for distribution in Africa. Our first stop was Nairobi, where we met Jomo Kenyatta, Kenya's president. Physically, he reminded me of Uncle Remus, but, carrying an ever present fly whisk, he was sharp and thoroughly enjoyed the ceremonies put on in his honor.

I was most impressed by Tanzania and Nigeria. Tanzania was experimenting with an African brand of socialism and Nigeria was such a huge country. The British left their mark on their former colonies. The civil service was patterned after the British system and so were the governments. But there was a glaring exception—most of the countries were one-party states. I didn't agree with this principle. How would there be enough room for dissent? Wouldn't you wind up with "strongmen" running everything and possibly becoming corrupt? I read Nyerere's book on African socialism and began to seriously question how countries were organized.

African students at the University of Dar es Salaam complained about the Asian shopkeepers, whom they accused of cheating them. For the first time, I felt unprepared for these confrontations. The same sort of reception happened to Muhammad Ali ten years later, but for different reasons.

There were questions: "What are you and other famous black Americans doing for the struggle in the U.S.?" "What do you think of the Vietnam War?" "Can you live any place you want?" "Did you know Dr. Martin Luther King, Jr.?" "When are you coming to Africa to show us how to play tennis?" Did I know Muhammad Ali? Stokely Carmichael? They were starved for information. Their main source about black America was *Ebony* and the VOA radio reports. When I turned the tables and started asking questions of my own, as I had with foreign students at UCLA, they also got defensive. "Why does your government lock up political prisoners? "Why can't you come up with an orderly way to change governments?" "Why does your government trade with South Africa?" Later, I was told that some people were afraid to answer my questions publicly; some of their activist friends had disappeared. I soon learned that the countries that screamed loudest about South Africa were farthest from it; in fact, trade between South Africa and black Africa is now increasing when one would have thought otherwise.

As an American, I was blamed for the ills of Africa.

Never mind that the United States never had colonies there: we were the whipping boy. But Africa was losing its best talents to lunatics—black and white. Tom M'Boya, touted as a future leader of Kenya, was assassinated—just like Martin and Malcolm. Nelson Mandela was jailed on South Africa's Robben Island. Robert Sobukwe was under house arrest. Many leaders of black Africa were despots, or corrupt, or both.

I was also told that as World War II drew to a close, there was serious talk of locating Israel in East Africa. The British entertained the idea, but the Zionists wouldn't hear of it. The notion floored me: imagine how divisive that arrangement would have been in the face of emerging African nationalism.

Of course, the African countries had their own divisions. Sometimes, even the most rudimentary courtesies between adjoining countries were missing. For example, getting a visa from Tanzania to Uganda was very difficult. Tribalism was a serious problem—the depth of the issue was staggering. Kenyatta was a Kikuyu; that meant his vice president had to be a Luo—something not unlike our balanced ethnic ticket in big-city politics.

The Africans told me my views were shortsighted, that I didn't take into account the legacy of colonialism and racism. "You Negroes in America are powerless. At least we have our own country." I heard that statement more than once.

In Lagos, Stan and I talked privately with General Yakabu Gowon, the military ruler of Nigeria. The Biafran War was not long over and the world was acutely aware of the number of military rulers in African countries. At the time, the army was probably the only entity strong enough to keep the peace. Gowon was a graduate of Sandhurst, the West Point of Great Britain. He laughed very easily, talked freely and spoke of the need to return Nigeria to civilian rule as soon as possible. "Nigeria feels a great kinship with Afro-Americans. We are the two most important groups of color in the world today. We have a great responsibility to Africa's descendants all over the world."

Despite his military background, Gowon talked like a statesman. I was surprised later to hear that he was deposed in a bloodless coup while away on official state business.

I returned from the African trip wiser but more confused, as I had been after my first trip to Southeast Asia, by the bombardment of cultures, people, politics, and the war. It took me a long time to sort out Vietnam and it would take me as long to deal with Africa, especially when it came to that nation where white supremacy reigned—the Republic of South Africa.

9

A Land of Promise?

I would love to serve as United States ambassador to South Africa. I'm sure the post would never be offered to me, but if it were, I would accept immediately. It would be a helluva challenge because I still believe that South Africa can be one of the great countries in the world. Their potential is enormous.

Technologically, South Africa is as advanced as West Germany, Switzerland, Israel, or Sweden. It has almost every natural resource known to man except oil, but it has the most hypocritical political system. It professes to be a Southern-Baptist-type Western civilization with Judeo-Christian philosophical morality; in reality, it practices the worst kind of discrimination. It has literally decided that the white European is there to govern, and there is a pecking order for everybody else. The pecking order starts at the top with the white Afrikaners, followed by the English-speaking whites, including the Jewish community. The Asians are at the top of the nonwhite section, then the Coloreds and the Africans at the bottom.

Many people have written off South Africa as hopeless. Not me. I don't believe the West is going to goad South Africa into change. In fact, the West does not want South Africa to change too much, because it wants the steady flow of natural resources from South Africa; so the change must come from within.

South Africa has more cobalt, magnesium, iron ore, coal, uranium, diamonds, and gold than it could ever use internally. It is also self-sufficient, producing more than enough food for its 26 million people. South Africa provides the United States and other Western countries with critically needed metals at a time when the balance of power in the world is very delicate. The Central Intelli-

gence Agency and the upper echelons in the State Department and Department of Defense seem convinced it is not
worth the effort to actively support a revolutionary movement in South Africa which may, in turn, lead to a black
takeover. In their minds, any takeover by a black majority
could turn all those natural resources into an OPEC-type
cartel. The West is scared to death of what might happen
if South African blacks got control of the government.
They're afraid that the blacks would emulate the Arabs
and jack up the prices on these natural resources or em-
bargo them for ransom.

The Arabs have a trump card with their oil. Most geol-
ogists and scientists believe that Arab oil may start peter-
ing out around the year 2000. Some of the natural
resources in South Africa come from a bottomless pit.
There is enough coal to last five hundred years, and there
is hydroelectric power. No matter how oppressive South
Africa's apartheid policy may be, a steady supply of gold,
cobalt and uranium is more important to the United
States, in the eyes of the CIA, than an unstable black African government. So the United States, having watched
other emerging black majorities struggle in Africa, pays
lip service to black aspirations in South Africa. Even if an
ultra-liberal president were elected, I'm certain the Penta-
gon and CIA would tell him or her, "Hey, shut up. We
need those natural resources, and we need a steady, unin-
terrupted stream. If a black government gets in, what's to
say that they won't do to those natural resources what the
Arabs did to us with their oil?"

We now give Israel almost $2 billion a year in aid. Some
Israelis want to think that our support is because the
United States likes Israel. That's not the reason. The reason is oil. If Israel were anyplace else, and it were in trouble, and there were no oil or natural resources nearby that
the West had to have to survive, Israel would not be getting that $2 billion, even with an effective Jewish lobby.

I became emotionally involved in South Africa as far

back as 1968, when Cliff Drysdale first told me that I had no chance of playing there. We had just finished a players' meeting at Queen's Club in London. Cliff and I were about to leave the club to catch a taxi when I pulled him aside.

"What are the chances of me playing in South Africa?" I asked.

"There are two things I can say about that," Cliff replied. "I think you have no chance of getting in now. And secondly, you have to keep in mind that the reason you can't get in is not because of the South African Lawn Tennis Union but because of the government. The government won't give you a visa. If the government gave you a visa, they would let you in the tournament."

I took Cliff at his word. Sort of. I waited until 1969 before quietly filing my visa application. Naturally, I was turned down, as Cliff had said. I was also turned down in 1970 without explanation. Donald Dell was more amazed than I was.

The second time I applied, I happened to be staying at Gladys Heldman's apartment. Gladys was the editor and publisher of *World Tennis* magazine at the time, and she loved a political fight. "You deserve to play," she told me. "Don't give up."

There was no intense feeling in the black community then on whether I should or should not go to South Africa. The debate began in 1973 when my visa was approved. That's when people said, "No, you shouldn't go. Why go all the way to South Africa for a cause when we've got problems right here?"

The late sixties and early seventies were the height of the black cultural revolution in the United States. We wore Afro hairdos and dashikis. Being as black as you could be at the time, culturally and mentally, was in vogue. I saw the South African situation from two levels: it was a place where the conditions for black people were much worse than in the United States, and I was personally being denied an opportunity to play in a tournament that, rightly or wrongly, was part of the international circuit. I felt I should have the right to play in this tournament or the tournament shouldn't have the right to be included in the ITF circuit.

It's easy to cop a plea and remain uninvolved on South Africa. Gary Player, a South African, says, "I'm a golfer, not a politician," when the media asks for his views. He's a hypocrite. I would like Gary Player to address himself to the question of whether he favors apartheid or not—a simple yes or no would suffice. But he won't answer the question. I'm sure if he says no, he might be run out of town or the government might stop giving him all the concessions he receives. Player is used by the South African government to extol the virtues of South Africa. The government would not use someone who is antiapartheid for this purpose.

I'm opposed though to a rule that would prohibit South African athletes from competing in the United States. But I believe Gary Player and other South Africans should be queried on their position toward apartheid. If they publicly renounce apartheid, they can play. If they support apartheid, then I would say the public can harass the hell out of them if it so chooses. It's similar to our situation regarding the bombing of Cambodia in 1969 and 1970. I had a few European players tell me at that time: "You people are nuts." I didn't bomb Cambodia. Nixon and Kissinger ordered the bombing. But I publicly disavowed what they did, so I felt blameless. If you give South African players a chance to publicly disavow what their government thinks, and if these players think apartheid is morally reprehensible, we've got to let them in.

The reason that the South African government let me in was because they were trying to change their image in the international community. They wanted to participate in the Olympics in a big way, and figured that admitting blacks like me was a way to demonstrate progress.

As a black athlete and black person, I knew I could not go to South Africa solely for athletic purposes. I had to go there, look around, absorb all I could about the place, and publicize my feelings. Most of what people in the United States know about South Africa is what they read in *The New York Times, Washington Post,* or learn from the wire services. Those stories are usually written by white people, even if they may be sensitive to the circumstances.

I feel I have some credibility in talking about South Africa. I was brought up under a similar situation, having lived in the segregated South. I have more feeling being black, intuitively, than some northerner who may live with a false feeling of integration. You can go to the same schools with someone but when you get right down to it, it's the society that counts. With the exception of Charles Diggs, the black congressman, few politicians were dealing with South Africa then on a permanent basis. My first trip to South Africa convinced me that I could play a significant role as far as raising the level of awareness within the white community both in South Africa and the United States.

Before I went to South Africa, I bought and read quite a few books on the history of the country, including some novels—even Henry Kissinger's secret memorandum on tilting American foreign policy toward South Africa. I wrote letters to Andrew Young, Sargent Shriver, J. D. Morgan, Bob Kelleher, and other friends and asked for opinions about the trip. By the time I arrived in Johannesburg in November 1973, I felt prepared to discuss apartheid.

I laid down three conditions for my visit and requested a response in writing from Piet Koornhof, the minister of immigration and sports: I wouldn't play before a segregated audience; I wouldn't come as an "honorary white," and I would be allowed to go where I pleased and say what I wanted. Surprisingly, he agreed.

The trip took on enormous proportions to me. Times had changed since 1969. People were vehemently for or against my going, and my intentions (and politics) generated considerable debate. When I stepped off the plane at Jan Smuts International Airport, my first reaction was to look for signs proclaiming South Africa's policy of separation. There were none. I was in the international terminal; since this was international territory, South Africa's laws of racial separation were suspended. Later I would find the laws (and the hateful signs) on the other side of the airport in the domestic terminal. If I wanted to go to a public bathroom in South Africa, I found that four choices existed: white ("blankes") and nonwhite ("nie-blankes"), male and female. Every public facility had four rest rooms. Many stores had separate entrances and divided counters, all in the interest of apartheid.

As we drove through the streets on the way to the home of our host, Brian Young, I saw no immediate evidence of apartheid. The only indication of racial arrangements was seeing blacks doing all the dirtiest, toughest, physical work. The most noticeable evidence was that almost all the pedestrians were black. Whites seemed to ride, and the only blacks in vehicles were chauffeurs and truck drivers.

Brian was a wealthy Jewish businessman, a member of a community in South Africa that is unabashedly liberal in its outlook, relatively speaking. It was ironic that on my first trip there, I should stay in the home of a Jewish liberal who reminded me of the people who had helped me or influenced my thinking at other stages of my career.

Once we got to Brian's home, Donald and Carole Dell, exhausted from the long trip, decided to take a nap. I was too excited to sleep, so I went out on the porch. At about 11:30 Anna, one of Brian's maids, came out, looked at me sideways and said, "What does the master want for lunch?"

It took me about five seconds to shake off the shock. I was completely caught off guard.

"Please don't call me master," I said. "You can call me Arthur."

She would not respond. She also continued to avert eye contact with me. I was reminded of the old South, when a black man looked away when listening to the instructions of a white man. Now I was in the role of the white man.

"I don't want them to call me master," I later told Brian. "Even 'sir' would be better than that."

"They won't do it," Brian answered. "I've tried to get them to call me Mr. Young, but they refuse. Wherever else they go, it's 'yes, master' or 'danke, bass.' "

Despite our rocky start, I eventually had long conversations with Brian's maid. She came from a town two hundred miles from "Jo'burg." I immediately understood the anguish and pain of family separation. She got to see her family only twice a year; she had no choice. There were no jobs in the bare dusty "homelands" set up by the government to make racial separation permanent. She beamed when I told her my stepmother had worked for a white family in Richmond. She didn't know where Richmond was but had romantic notions about America that reminded me of my naive ideals about California before I saw it. She could read and write and followed my matches in the newspapers very closely. On my last day she called me Arthur.

For my appearance the rules were changed at Ellis Park, site of the tournament, to meet my conditions, but the signs were still up: "Blankes-Whites-Europeans" and Nieblankes-Nonwhites-Non-Europeans." I still reacted strongly to the signs. "It really is true," I said to myself. "These people are nuts."

When I played, the nonwhite section was jammed with Africans. There was a railing on either side of this section to cordon it off, but the promoter, Owen Williams, had

150

The first of Ashe's two solid-gold tennis balls on the
WCT tour, 1975. (Wide World Photos)

Receiving the 1975 WCT trophy from John Connally.
(Wide World Photos)

Wimbledon, 1975, with Jimmy Connors. (Wide World Photos)

How sweet it is! Wimbledon, 1975. (Russ Adams)

Ashe's wedding; with Andrew Young officiating, brother Johnnie to
Ashe's right, and Jeanne's friend Diane Elliston to her left.
(Wide World Photos)

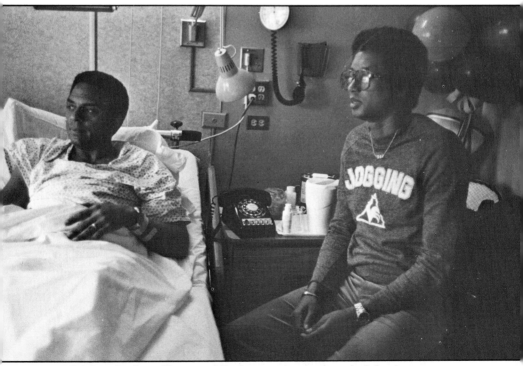

Visiting Andrew Young while he was in the hospital for leg
surgery. (Jeanne Moutoussamy-Ashe)

Ashe as chairman of the National Easter Seal
Sports Council, with Kristin Behrmann.

Receiving an award from King Carl of Sweden (right).
(Jacob Forsell/*Expressen*, Stockholm)

With grandmother Amelia Johnson Ashe Taylor.
(Jeanne Moutoussamy-Ashe)

The Ashe family reunion, 1977. (Jeanne Moutoussamy-Ashe)

South Africa. (Jeanne Moutoussamy-Ashe)

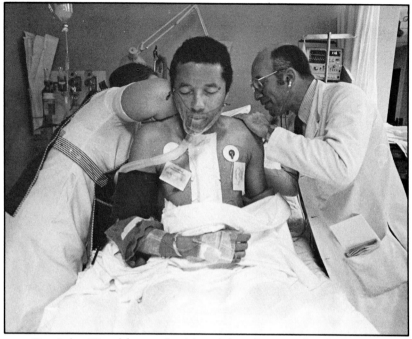

Dr. John Hutchinson checking Ashe after quadruple by-pass
surgery in 1979. (Jeanne Moutoussamy-Ashe)

Arthur Ashe and friends: Top, left to right:
Dennis Ralston, Tom Gorman, Brian Gottfried, Ashe, Bob Lutz,
Charles Pasarell; bottom, left to right: Frank Craighill,
Stan Smith, Dick Stockton, Roscoe Tanner, Marty Riessen,
Donald Dell. (Jeanne Moutoussamy-Ashe)

Arthur and Jeanne.

In his den, New York City, 1978. (Jeanne Moutoussamy-Ashe)

obtained permission to have Africans, Asians, and Coloreds sit in seats they had been barred from before. This
may not seem like much to black Americans, but it had
major significance in the South African scheme of things.

I saw a "force" in the faces of the black spectators that
helped my game. When I played Bob Hewitt in the quarterfinals, the Africans were beside themselves. They
shouldn't have cheered Hewitt's mistakes, but I understood their feelings. It was comparable to some of my
black friends talking about "those white boys" during my
junior days, an opportunity to defy the system; in South
Africa, there are few ways for black South Africans to
make that kind of statement.

I was semi-satisfied with my tennis performance. I lost
to Jimmy Connors in the final, 6–4, 7–6, 6–3, but I won
the doubles with Tom Okker, 6–2, 4–6, 6–4. A black
man's name was on the champion's board at Ellis Park.

As usual, activities off the court intrigued me more. I
wanted to see and do everything. I wanted to visit every
tribe, talk to everybody, find out firsthand how this bastion
of Western civilization could still fervently believe in apartheid.

I talked to Dr. Piet Koornhof. He was widely regarded
as the most liberal member of the cabinet and a possible
future prime minister. Dr. Koornhof didn't want me to
quote our conversation—just to use its general content.
He said he was aware of international pressures but that
South Africa was trying to solve its problems its own way
and that pressures only made things worse. He objected to
what he called a "double standard" that made it right for
other countries to violate the rights of their citizens while
South Africa was singled out.

"No other country except Rhodesia has laws that categorize and separate its people by race," I tried to tell him.
The conversation was friendly, but Dr. Koornhof didn't
answer many of my questions directly. He skirted issues

151

and became philosophical. He seemed sympathetic to the plight of blacks but stopped short of saying that apartheid was wrong. He offered almost no hope of one-man, one-vote rule. So much for Western civilization.

My relationship with most South African tennis players has always been good. Ray Moore and Cliff Drysdale were openly critical of apartheid. Their attitudes were more typical of the rule for South African players, even though most of them were not so open about their feelings. Bob Hewitt, who was originally from Australia but had lived for a long time in South Africa, never said much. He did once tell me that black Africans were happy in South Africa; I was offended by his paternalism and condescension, but concluded it had to do with a lack of exposure rather than a racist attitude. He helped me with a fund-raising benefit for the Black Tennis Foundation there.

In Capetown, where there is a large Colored population, Donald and I met with an anthropology professor and three graduate students at Stellenbosch University, the "Harvard of South Africa." Stellenbosch, a haven for Afrikaners, has produced all the country's prime ministers. As we talked, I was amazed that a learned man with a Ph.D. could genuinely believe that apartheid was just and moral.

"You are an exception," he told me. "You are not completely black; you have some white blood in you."

Political science professors and government service people here in the United States may know more about South Africa, in an intricate way, than I do. But in five visits there, I have driven around the country, talked to more people, and have a better feel for what is going on there than those professors. I am disliked by both the extreme right of the White Nationalist Party and the extreme black left, and there aren't many who can make that claim.

The black leftists assume that my presence lends credence to the government; they want total isolation of the white-dominated government—no cultural exchanges, no business, no nothing—just leave South Africa alone but try from the outside, through the United Nations or other means, to get companies to pull out.

The far right doesn't want me there because they preach strict adherence to the rules of apartheid. Strict rules means that if you are black, you can't come in.

Obviously, I don't know where apartheid is going to lead. But I'm convinced that the change is going to come from within and it's going to take a while because organization is difficult for the liberation movements there. Not even all the black people there can talk to one another. They don't all speak the same language. On the one hand, some black intellectuals don't want the American multinational corporation to pull out because some tribes might lose jobs that way. Then there are other blacks who say, "Instead of having these companies pull out, I would rather have you exert pressure on the companies through the UN."

Tribal distinctions don't help the cause of unity, and my definition of education needed constant rethinking during my visits to South Africa. In their school system, white children must attend school, and it is free; black children are not required to attend and must pay.

The Afrikaners firmly believe that "colored peoples of the world all inherited the curse of Ham," and therefore are suited to be "tillers of the soil and hewers of wood." The Afrikaners lost the Boer War, but they eventually outnumbered the English-speaking South African whites and took political control of the country in 1948. While the Afrikaners may dislike their English-speaking countrymen, they want nothing to do socially with the "kaffirs," their equivalent term for "nigger." The Afrikaners have gone farther than American whites ever did on racial separation on the grounds that "God had decreed that the world runs better when group homogeneity is maintained."

South Africans are divided into four major races—

White, Asian, Colored, and African—but blacks are sub-divided into nine tribes, while whites are not. The Coloreds are perhaps the most alienated, since they are classified as neither white nor black.

I had one peculiar run-in in South Africa that reminded me of the way nonwhite South Africans had been divided. At a "Colored" social function that Andrew Young, Dr. Robert Green, and I attended, a man took me aside.

"You're spending a lot of time with the Africans and that's fine, but when are you going to help us a bit?" he said, quite vehemently.

I mumbled something about how Americans didn't differentiate between gradations of color. If you were black, you were black, no matter what shade. My reasoning didn't impress him.

"Hell," he said, "you're colored yourself. You should help your own kind."

M. N. Pather, an Asian, was the leader of the nonracial sports movement. His passport had been taken away to prevent him from arguing his case overseas. Pather argues that all white South African teams should be banned from international competition and that his group should be recognized as the legitimate sports organization for South Africa. Pather was one of the many people I met with incredible courage to stand up to the machinery of apartheid.

Another was Don Mattera, a Colored poet who was under a banning order. That meant certain jobs were off-limits to him, that nothing he said or wrote could be published, and that he could not attend meetings of more than two people for five years. I met Don during a session at Ellis Park just before I went to meet a group of black journalists at the USIS office. We talked for a long time, and I invited him to come to the meeting.

"I'm sorry, brother," he said, "I can't come up. It's against my banning orders." He had to stand in the street outside the USIS when I went into the building. The very fact that I mention Don's name in this book is enough to get it banned in South Africa.

I was unprepared for the reception black journalists gave me. Some had been drinking, and the meeting became an emotional confrontation.

"What role did you play in the civil rights struggle in the United States?"

"Were you in the 1963 march on Washington?"

"You black Americans think you can compare our situation with your struggle in America, and you can't."

They wanted to know what I thought of U.S. corporate investment in South Africa. How did I stand on the Olympic boycott of South Africa? Did I think that Ellis Park had really been integrated? Wasn't Owen Williams really a hypocrite?

I didn't lose my temper. The questions were fascinating and the passion behind the statements moving. I was more in awe of the depth of their emotions than the subject of the questions. This was one of the few places they could meet in public and vent some of their anger. "I came to South Africa because I wanted to see for myself what is going on," I said.

My answers had little impact and they accused me of being a "tool of the South African government."

"I don't have the answers," I said. "I'm just trying to find out for myself."

Another blatantly physical confrontation with the militant side took place when I gave a tennis clinic in Soweto. Several young black men accosted me afterward and began to denounce me as a "sellout and a stooge." They were incensed. After my visit with the journalists, I was prepared for emotional outbursts, but I sensed real rage here. The confrontation reminded me of the frustrations of black-on-black crime. Who else could these black youths get mad at and get away with it? The discussion got pretty heavy; later, Donald admitted he had been concerned for my safety. I wasn't, because I assumed that BOSS (Bureau of State Security) was watching anyway.

Jeanne had a similarly harrowing experience in 1977, when I went back to do a documentary for ABC's *Wide World of Sports*. She went to the train station in Johannesburg with a friend, Yusef Surtee, to watch people on the way home to Soweto. As she started to take pictures, a policeman came up, grabbed her arm and said, "Come with me, I have a few questions to ask you." When Jeanne opened her mouth and the policeman heard her American accent, he let her go and walked away.

Jeanne walked to a platform and started shooting again, but some of the Africans became quite upset. There is considerable suspicion about BOSS, and many believe that one out of four persons in Soweto is an informer. Jeanne wanted to get on the train and ride to the next stop. She didn't realize that she didn't belong on the train. She looks Asian or Colored, but not African. When she stepped on the train, the passengers took offense and started shouting at her. They pushed her, but she couldn't get off the train. After about ten seconds, the door suddenly opened again and she was shoved out by the angry passengers. Later, she learned that she had been quite lucky because the train made no stops until it got to Soweto. Jeanne was still shaking when she got back to Owen and Jennifer Williams's house.

Soweto was on the verge of coming apart in 1975. You could not tell by looking around at the streets. You had to talk to people. Black people were bolder about the things they didn't like; they were more vocally open. There were small, scattered disturbances that the police didn't seem to deal with harshly, disruptions at work sites that struck at the heart of how a man can live.

In 1973, minor social changes were made to Ellis Park; in 1974 more changes were made, and a liberalization pattern had begun in the sports structure; in 1975, there were more cosmetic changes, but you could feel the tension underneath. The superficial changes in petty apartheid only whetted the appetites of black South Africans for more and faster change. President Nixon was still in the White House, so South Africa was treated with a hands-off policy. But the fears that black journalists spoke about at that first meeting in 1973 and warned us about one year later broke through on June 16, 1976. Soweto erupted just as Watts and Newark had years before. Reading the news in the International Herald Tribune in London, I called Ray Moore at 8 A.M., woke him up, and said, "I told you so." He didn't believe it until be read it with his own eyes.

Even as the riots erupted, however, one startling, sobering statistic fascinated me: in all of the racial unrest, not even a handful of white South Africans were killed. The Africans talk in symbolic terms of destroying the system they hate, yet almost no white South Africans were killed. That wouldn't happen in the United States under similar circumstances. South African blacks were punishing themselves more than anybody else. Even when they had those riots, nobody in the lines had any weapons; the people were all unarmed, with nothing more than sticks and stones.

But that one incident changed values within the country. To all South Africans it meant that communications had improved within the black community more than expected. There was more unanimity of feeling about apartheid. The black reaction also showed that blacks were not going to settle for the life that white South Africa had been promising them. And, most important, South Africa internationally could no longer hide from the problem as it tried to do in the past. Even the investment atmosphere changed. Outsiders like me also had to change our approach. We could not rely on an occasional letter to a congressman or senator. We too had to raise our ante. I had to get bolder just to keep up.

There are two or three methods for involvement in

South Africa. People who have a point to make could buy some stock in a multinational company doing business there and then go to a stockholders' meeting, demand to be heard, and make their point. In fact, Patricia Harris, the former secretary of Health, Education and Welfare, was on the board of IBM. It's not just that a black woman is on the board; the important factor is that we can have a voice there, and the companies don't like to be embarrassed at annual meetings. Another way is to put pressure on companies through the Sullivan Manifesto, a code of ethics for multinational corporations doing business in South Africa. I have deep ties to TransAfrica, a predominantly black lobby group in the United States that was started four years ago and seeks to influence foreign policy vis-à-vis Africa. The executive director of TransAfrica is Randall Robinson, Max Robinson's brother, whom I grew up with in Richmond. He is a Harvard Law School graduate who is married to one of my childhood girl-friends, Brenda Randolph. We needed a lobby group to research Afro-American problems from a black perspective and to serve as a focal point. TransAfrica arose in direct response to the riots as well as reflecting a heightened awareness to what was going on there.

There were always episodes about South Africa that touched me deeply. As we were going through customs to leave after our first trip, a black man approached Carole Dell in the newspaper shop of the airport.

"I know you are traveling with Mr. Ashe," he said. "I want to get a message to him but I cannot be seen talking directly to him. I'm going to slip something inside a newspaper and have someone casually sit down next to you in the waiting room. Would you pick up this newspaper and give it to Mr. Ashe once you're on board?"

Carole was surprised but managed to say, "O.K."

Soon afterward, a man sat next to her in the waiting room and left a paper on the seat between them. Carole picked it up and carried it aboard.

A Land of Promise?

When I opened the newspaper, there was a picture of Winnie Mandela, wife of Nelson Mandela, the black leader who is serving a life sentence on Robben Island off the coast from Cape Town. On the back was a note thanking me for what I was trying to do but stating that neither I nor any other black American should assume that we could do the thinking of black South Africans for them. "The best you can do," she wrote, "is ask the South Africans what you can do to help in their struggle."

I felt strange touching down at JFK and reentering the "real world." My stomach had been knotted the entire time and I was tense and taut. It was incredible that people still thought in terms of racial supremacy. Wasn't the Holocaust of World War II enough to discredit any notion of ethnic superiority? I always thought the Holocaust and Neil Armstrong's walking on the moon to be the two most significant events in my lifetime so far.

In addition to the tournament there, my effort to grapple with the ethos of South Africans was the main reason I kept going back. Each time, I met more people, understood more, and struggled to refine my own conclusions about the country.

The most impressive encounter was with Robert Sobukwe, the late South African activist, who was hounded in and out of jail until his death in 1978. Mr. Sobukwe headed the Pan-African Congress in South Africa. He was jailed for his protests of South Africa's racial laws and spent time in solitary confinement. Like his African National Congress counterpart, Nelson Mandela, Sobukwe never compromised his principles.

On my 1974 trip, Dr. Robert Green, dean of the College of Urban Affairs at Michigan State; Michael Cardoza, Donald's assistant; and Andrew Young came along. We made arrangements to see Sobukwe in Kimberley, the diamond-mining center of South Africa. He had just become a lawyer but was still under a form of house arrest. This meant that he had to be in his house from 6:00 P.M. until

159

6:00 A.M. every weekday and from 6:00 P.M. on Friday until 6:00 A.M. the following Monday. Under no circumstances could he leave Kimberley. Andy, Michael, and I flew to see him and in essence broke the law (from Sobukwe's standpoint) by meeting with him. Like Don Mattera, Sobukwe was not allowed to meet with more than two non-family members at one time.

Sobukwe welcomed us warmly, offered us coffee, and thanked us for making the trip. "I've been following your exploits in the press here. It is indeed a great pleasure to meet you, Mr. Young," he said. "We all think highly of you, Dr. King, and the movement he started."

I asked Sobukwe how he was faring and whether he thought my trip to South Africa was good for black South Africans. With that question, he launched into an hour-long discussion on South African race relations and the role of the outside world in bringing about equality. Andy, Michael, and I just listened for sixty minutes.

Sobukwe was not angry or bitter. "A lot of good could result from your trip," he said. "We have many problems here and not too many black Americans really know our situation. If you could help explain our predicament to your countrymen, that in itself would be a help."

His statement was all the support I needed for critics back in the United States who contended I shouldn't go for any reason.

Yusef Surtee, an Asian, became a very good friend. His family runs several large clothing stores, and Yusef has a large comfortable house in Lenasia (the word is a contraction of "land for Asians") in an area half as far from Johannesburg as Soweto. He also keeps an apartment in Johannesburg, right across the street from a large police station.

Yusef was well connected in South African business circles and assisted Owen Williams in setting up a chat for me with Harry Oppenheimer, who may be the country's most famous businessman. Oppenheimer has been an advocate of doing away with job reservation laws, which preserve certain job categories for whites, and he has made efforts to improve the lot of black workers in the enterprises he controls. He heads the Urban Foundation, which directs corporate funds to worthwhile projects in nonwhite sectors.

Oppenheimer and other progressive businessmen work through the American Chamber of Commerce of South Africa, which adopted the so-called Sullivan principles several years ago. The Sullivan principles, put forward by the Reverend Leon Sullivan, a black minister who is a board member of General Motors, sets guidelines for treatment of black workers. The rules are voluntary and have had only moderate success. I am disappointed in the results so far. Foreign business people try to say they are working well, but in private they will admit, "We're just doing whatever we can to make as much profit as we can and we're going to stick our necks out only so far. The government might ask us to leave."

During my second trip to South Africa, I visited Dr. Christiaan Barnard, the heart specialist, at Groote Schur Hospital in Cape Town. Although by birth he is an English-speaking South African with supposedly liberal views about apartheid, I had doubts about his racial attitudes. Hell, I had doubts about all white South Africans. He was a great heart surgeon, an innovator, an acknowledged expert in his field. Yet apartheid is so overwhelming that problems of race cloud every issue in South Africa.

"We don't discriminate here," he began, as he showed me the cardiac clinic. There, indeed, in a special section of the hospital, were a black baby and white baby side-by-side —both with congenital heart defects. Dr. Barnard's statement was very revealing; he said it as if it was the right thing to do and his government was wrong.

"But I do not believe yet in one-man one-vote in South

Africa," he went on, in a practical conclusion he said he had come to after having traveled quite a bit. If a "liberal" like Barnard doesn't go along with one-man, one-vote, South Africa has a long way to go. An implicit quota system loomed in the back of Barnard's mind. He believed logically that all men were equal, but evidence led him to the conclusion that his country would be better off not immediately putting the ballot in the hands of his African maid or his illiterate gardener.

Those who claim there is white support for equality inside South Africa exaggerate their claims. The white liberals there are not as liberal as they'd have you believe— Jews included. They realize that they owe their high standard of living to the artificially cheap indigenous black labor. Owen, his wife Jennifer, Jeanne, and I had conversations about whether "liberals" like Owen should stay and try to change their country or leave out of disgust. Owen has decided to stay—for now.

Since that conversation with Dr. Barnard, I have come to the conclusion that white South Africa will have to be forced to change.

I have spent most of my adult life around white people. Even today, about one-half of my friends are white. Conversely, my youth was spent around black people. White people were to be deferred to, respected. At least, so I thought while growing up. The first whites I got to know —the insurance collectors, the Thalhimers, the Schillers, the Schwarzschilds—were nice people, so my first impression of whites was positive.

But I soon learned that, collectively, white people didn't really like blacks. They kept us from going to school with them, worshipping with them, playing with them. It was not difficult to place the blame on them for the discrimination that black people had to suffer. Whites were at fault. I knew that and was bitter toward white Richmond after I left. For a long time, I recoiled at the sound of a southern accent; it reminded me of the Louisville Boat Club or the Country Club of Virginia, of not being able to play in the State Jaycees, of being turned away at Byrd Park.

I have always resisted the notion of a blanket condemnation of white people—or any other group of people. That just cannot work. I wouldn't want anyone lumping me in some blanket generalization about black people. Only time and trust tell the story. I use this same reasoning when I adamantly refuse to place the sins of the South African government on South African tennis players and athletes. I couldn't refuse a South African the right to earn a living playing in the United States—as long as he or she disavows apartheid.

At the same time, it is difficult not to react to South African beliefs about race with hate; that was my first reaction. But the more I learned about white South Africans, the more I understood how useless it was to hate them. It's not what people think that is important, but what they believe; it's a matter of turning those beliefs around. White South Africans really believe they are right and the rest of the world wrong.

In 1965, Ian Smith assumed the prime ministership of Rhodesia and issued a UDI, or Unilateral Declaration of Independence, from Great Britain. As South Africa's chief African ally, Prime Minister Smith was vilified throughout much of the world. His son Alex was so alienated by what his father did that for years they rarely spoke.

I met Alex in the London home of Bunny Austin, a former Wimbledon champion, in 1977. Alex spoke of the tremendous guilt he felt in going against his father and learning that his father was a racist. "It pained me no end to know that my father was the leader of this little band of white racists," he said. "They were raised with the colonialist's mentality and were victims of their environment. I knew he was wrong and I had to weigh the pain of

163

alienation against the guilt of siding with him. I decided I had to do the morally right thing. My father was wrong."

I had many chats at Bunny's house over the years, but none quite so fascinating. I followed the fortunes of South Africa and Rhodesia in all the magazines and newspapers, and here was the scion of a man I had come to despise.

"My father will fight to the end to defend white privilege in Rhodesia," Alex said at the time. "He really believes he is doing the right thing, that the African must be cared for rather than be the caretaker. The biggest thing he has going for him is that he is anticommunist. You Americans are paranoid about communism, so you left him alone."

Alex saw the writing on the wall. He didn't guess that Robert Mugabe would be elected in a "freely held" election, but it happened anyway. "You Americans are losing friends in the Third World because you come down on the wrong side with too little too late," he said. "Angola is a perfect example; Mozambique also. Neither country was definitely headed toward a Marxist form of government. You let it slip away, all because you are so scared of communism. Racism for these Africans is a lot more oppressive than communism."

There are parallels between the racial progress we've made in the United States and the issues in South Africa. Bobby Kennedy once went to South Africa and opened with this statement: "I want to talk about a country where the Dutch settled, displaced the local population and imposed their culture. I'm talking about the United States of America."

There is little outrage among white Americans about South Africa because the business lobby is too strong. There is no effective antiapartheid lobby. To business, South Africa is a place that returns an average 19 percent profit on investment. The fact that cheap black labor makes this possible is not an issue.

I could muster enough of a fuss to almost ruin the South

African Open. I don't do it because I don't want the door to be shut completely on communication, and tennis is one of the more progressive sports in the country. Tennis and cricket have opened doors for South African blacks in other sports.

South African blacks need positive role models. There are few living heroes because they are killed or imprisoned. We must encourage the "verligtes" (the enlightened Afrikaners) and create an atmosphere that brings about change without the government losing face.

As a result of my 1973 trip, Owen Williams and I started the Black Tennis Foundation. Now there is the Javabu Tennis Complex in Soweto with eight tennis courts. It will soon have a clubhouse and enough amenities to serve as a social meeting place as well. Some teams have been started, and I believe it will pay off in new players in the years ahead.

But I draw the line at the so-called South African homelands. These phony countries set up by the government represent the disenfranchisement of black South Africans. The Transkei and Bophutatswana and Vendaland concepts should be discouraged and dismantled as soon as possible. They will never work, and some white South Africans are beginning to realize this.

Urban guerrilla violence will continue in South Africa. I can't foresee an all-out war or coup. South Africa is surrounded by vast stretches of wasteland that preclude surprise attack. Real military struggle requires coordination and communication efforts that are presently beyond the immediate capacity of opponents of the government.

Informers are also an anti-revolutionary tool for the government against revolution. This works well because the government pays well for information. And in a country where there is not enough work, and real hunger, people will do things like this for money.

The resistance to apartheid comes mostly from the

young. Those over forty have been brainwashed and feel so inferior that they are only marginally willing to put up a fuss. Nonwhites who have achieved some material gains, like those elsewhere, are very conservative.

Much of black Africa believes that if push came to shove in South Africa, the United States would side with the white-minority government there. Many Africans were genuinely surprised that we ceded the Panama Canal to the Panamanians; it was an indication that we were trying to change after all.

I am not for disinvestment from South Africa by American companies if they meet the prescribed hiring goals. I feel this for two practical reasons. (a) Economic power will precede major advances in other areas. What the white South African abhors most is the notion of having to integrate with someone he sees as indigent. He will put up less resistance to mixing with people of means, no matter what their color. For this, jobs are needed—every job possible. (b) Disinvestment won't work. It is a noble idea that will not come to pass, there is no power around strong enough to force it. If and when black Africa starts flexing its muscle on the South African issue, the result is more apt to be "stay there and do the right thing" rather than "pull out." Oddly, black African trade with South Africa shows no signs of stopping. But that doesn't mean we should soften our stand on apartheid.

10

Wimbledon 1975

The words blurted out naturally, as if they had been recorded in my mind. "I have this funny feeling I can't lose," I told Dr. Doug Stein as we ate breakfast at the Westbury Hotel.

I wasn't sure whether Doug would laugh or cry. The whole world was betting on Jimmy Connors to continue his march through Wimbledon and win another title. And here I was, on the morning of the 1975 men's singles final, telling one of my best friends that I couldn't lose.

Doug looked at me and smiled. He was a first-year surgical resident at the time and understood the value of positive thinking. "Terrific," he said. "That's the way to think."

I smiled, in between a sip of tea. "Don't laugh," Doug continued, in a very emphatic manner that I have come to understand and respect. "Look, it's been proven without a doubt. In my field, people who have a positive attitude heal faster. I mean you can literally fight for your life, and if you want to live strongly enough, you might come through difficult times. If you think, 'Hey, I'm really going to win today, or I'm going to play well,' and you really feel it, you probably will play better than you normally play."

I wasn't sure whether Doug was trying to pump me up or prepare me for what everybody saw as the inevitable. After all, Jimmy Connors was running the show the way Rod Laver had a decade earlier. In 1974, Connors had one of the greatest years anyone could recall, winning the Australian, Wimbledon, and U.S. Open titles. The only reason he didn't win Paris was because the French had barred him because of his contractual ties with World Team Tennis. Connors won fifteen tournaments that year and set a modern record by winning 96 percent of his singles matches—99 of 103. His only losses were to Karl Meiler, Stan Smith, Onny Parun, and Juan Gisbert. My record in 1974 was 85–27, which was a pretty healthy .759. But it palled alongside Connors's stats for the season, and Jimmy picked up where he left off at Wimbledon by beating John Lloyd, Vijay Amritraj, Mark Cox, Phil Dent, Raul Ramirez, and Roscoe Tanner in straight sets.

Betting is legal in England. On the day of our final, Hills bookmakers had made Jimmy 3 to 20 to win and 9 to 10 to win in straight sets. I was definitely a long shot, to say the least. Anyone who thought I could win in straight sets got 40 to 1 odds.

One of the persistent comments about me in 1974 was that I was always a bridesmaid. I had reached the finals of eleven tournaments but won only two. Some members of the media said I was spending too much time on the administrative side of tennis or with my business ventures and wasn't singleminded enough to get the job done properly. At the time, I resented the criticism; in hindsight, I must admit that my critics were partly right. I was involved in too many things to concentrate on my game. I was president of the Association of Tennis Professionals and very involved with the politics of the game. I needed an approach similar to Bjorn Borg's. Borg has a coach, Lennart Bergelin, and a manager, Bob Kain from the International Management Group, and all he has to worry about is hitting the tennis ball. But I knew that I would go nuts if I only played tennis, so there were compromises I had to make for peace of mind.

In 1975, I decided to start off the year in tiptop shape. I remembered how the weight-training program I had taken during the winter of 1967 at West Point had contributed to my great year in 1968. So I took off for Puerto Rico with a few friends and Henry Hines, the world-class long jumper, whom I had met the year before. Henry had watched us practice a few times and suggested ways to improve our footwork and conditioning. He felt that tennis players could be 50 percent more effective physically by preparing more carefully.

The World Championship Tennis season started well for me. My only problem, aside from facing Borg in three early tournaments that winter, was some pain in my left heel. I started to walk with a slight limp, but the pain went away after a warmup of about five minutes and didn't bother me until I took a shower after a match. Since I was approaching my thirty-second birthday, I attributed the pains to aging.

My confidence soared when I beat Borg in the WCT finals in Dallas. The year before, John Newcombe had received $25,000 in a wheelbarrow after winning the WCT final over Borg. My $33,333.33 first prize came in the shape of a pure 24-karat gold tennis ball. In those days, gold was considerably less expensive than it is now. In fact, they actually had more gold than they could fit in the sphere of a tennis ball, so they used the rest to make a pedestal of solid gold. When I won the Haggar bonus pool set up by WCT, the price of gold was about $119 an ounce. That gold tennis ball is now worth about $125,000.

Winning WCT made me think about Wimbledon. Much of the decorum had gone out of tennis, and the respect for tradition that was promoted by Laver, Rosewall, Emerson, and the other Aussies was fading. But Wimbledon remained special. Players might try to get away with something at any other event on the tour, even Forest Hills, but they were on good behavior at Wimbledon.

I had reached the semifinals at Wimbledon in 1968 and 1969, each time losing to—who else?—Laver. The odds were against me in the French and Italian Opens because of their clay courts and Borg's emergence. I had won the U.S. Open in 1968 and the Australian in 1970, both on grass courts. Even with Connors at the top of his game, my mental state was never better for a run at Wimbledon.

My usual routine in the spring was to play the European

clay-court circuit and work my way to England. This time, I entered the Italian, but skipped the French and instead played the grass circuit in England. I won Beckenham, lost to Tony Roche at Nottingham, but was pleased with my game. I felt ready.

Players prepare meticulously for Wimbledon. They want to do everything that can help their tennis. They want to feel well, stay somewhere without distractions or annoyances, and avoid getting their food late or missing limousine rides to the courts. I stayed at my favorite overseas hotel, the Westbury. They would take good care of me.

I ran down the list of checkpoints I carried in my head. I had done well all year, I felt fit. My foot problem was there, but I knew how to handle it. Mentally, the important thing was to get through the first week. Too many good players lose in the early rounds because they're looking ahead to more important matches.

I was seeded sixth in the tournament and drew the ideal schedule: matches on Monday, Wednesday, Thursday, and Saturday. My first-round opponent was Bob Hewitt. I won, 7–5, 3–6, 6–2, 6–4. I had another fairly easy match in the second round, 6–2, 7–5, 6–4, over Japan's Jun Kamiwazumi.

I had reached the third round losing only one set, a statistic that could become important. I wanted to get out of the first few rounds with as few lost sets as possible. If I had to struggle, I could get tired and not play my best in the later rounds. My third-round opponent was Brian Gottfried. He provided my first real test because he was a solid player, but Brian had never caused a great deal of trouble for me except for a loss to him once in Las Vegas, and I won, 6–2, 6–3, 6–1 on Court 2. I felt a tremendous boost from such an easy win. I was in the fourth round and had lost just one set.

The draw also was working in my favor. I was scheduled

to play John Alexander of Australia, who was the tenth seed and a strong server on grass, but he was upset by an unseeded British pro, Graham Stilwell. On a misty Saturday, I met Stilwell on Court 1, my favorite, and won, 6–2, 5–7, 6–4, 6–2. I then got two days off as the men didn't play again until Tuesday.

My opponent in the quarters was Borg. I was fortunate that he was not yet the player he would be one day. Down a set, trailing, 3–0, in the second and in deep trouble, I came back to beat him 2–6, 6–4, 8–6, 6–1. The ending of the match was as strange as our earlier match in Dallas. He seemed to "give" a little when behind. I was surprised but wasn't going to complain. I had reached the semifinals.

On the other side of the draw, Roscoe Tanner and Connors had broken through. Roscoe had only lost one set up to the quarters, and he had beaten Guillermo Vilas in five sets.

My semifinal opponent was Tony Roche, who was seeded sixteenth. Tony had beaten Rosewall, the second seed, in the fourth round and Okker in five sets in the quarterfinals. We had a helluva match. He was left-handed and made me work hard, but I pulled it out, 5–7, 6–4, 7–5, 8–9, 6–4. In the other semifinal, I had never seen Roscoe serve better, but he won just nine games as Jimmy routed him, 6–4, 6–1, 6–4. Jimmy's returns, his control and power just overwhelmed Roscoe. As I watched the match, I knew that if I played my game I would lose.

The night before the final, I sat down at the Westbury with Dennis Ralston, Erik Van Dillen, Donald Dell, Marty Riessen, and Charlie Pasarell to figure out what I should do. I also saw Freddie McNair. Freddie was never a great player, better in doubles than singles. But we had been pals on the tour, and he knew my game fairly well.

"You've got to play through his strengths to his weaknesses," Freddie stressed.

"That's easy enough to say," I countered.

Donald offered his opinion. "You can do it if you put your mind to it. But it involves changing your style of play."

We broke down Jimmy's game, shot by shot. His major weakness was the low forehand approach shot. Also he liked pace, and he loved opening up the court hitting cross-court. If you tried to open up the court, he would try to open it wider. I had to go wide on both sides with my serves and keep as many balls as possible down the middle. Keep the ball low. And pray.

"Chip the ball," Dennis advised. "Don't hit over. Chip it. You want to make him hit up all the time."

I could hit a slice forehand. But sliced forehands were a shot that players used in the 1920s; we saw it more at the club level, on clay courts, than on the tour. But I knew I could use the sliced forehand if I had to. I also had a backhand slice, and I made up my mind that slices were going to be my bread-and-butter shots. Most of the time I would serve wide to Jimmy's backhand on the forehand court, serve wide to his forehand on the backhand court. When he served, I would chip the ball down the middle and short because the grass was worn down the middle, the ball wasn't going to bounce very high. If the ball was not higher than the height of the net, Jimmy couldn't hit down on it; he had to hit up on it. That meant he couldn't get as good an angle. If he came to the net, I would lob to his backhand side.

"Don't hit the ball hard," Dennis reminded. "No pace. No pace."

I would like to report that I went to bed at nine o'clock that night. But after our little get-together, we went to the Playboy Club, for dinner with one of the managers, John Willoughan. I tried a few hands of blackjack, called it quits about twelve-thirty, and was in bed about one o'clock. That was my usual routine. I'm not like my father, who is up at six-thirty every morning. I like to stay up late and get up late. Donald had always tried to get me to go to bed earlier and get up earlier. But at a place like Wimbledon, when you're worried about matches, the more time you have to think, the more nervous you get. At Wimbledon, starting time is two o'clock, so if you get up at nine you have five hours to wake up and get your juices flowing. Of course, it was different at the French or U.S. Opens, where play started at eleven in the morning. We had to get up at least three hours before a match to make sure we could be in fourth gear when we walked on the court.

For the first two sets against Jimmy, I must have been in fifth gear. I served well, carried out my game plan, and he made a lot of errors. What really surprised me, aside from winning the first two sets, 6–1, 6–1, was that I wasn't nervous. It was now 2:41 P.M. Maybe it was because nobody expected me to win. I'm sure that people thought I'd come out, play my game, and get blown off the court. But I was just shutting out all distractions and thinking about what I would do next.

There were enough distractions. Jimmy and I were not exactly chummy. Almost on the eve of Wimbledon, he announced that he was suing me for $3 million, charging libel and slander. It was another aftermath of Connors being led down the antiestablishment road by Bill Riordan, his manager at the time.

I had very little to do with Jimmy then. The only real conversation I had with him was on the porch at the Longwood Cricket Club the preceding summer when I tried to convince him to join ATP. Jimmy sat down, listened, and said he would consider it. Nothing ever came of it, and I didn't push matters. I was aware of Riordan's influence and the important role of Jimmy's mother, but I could identify with his outlook on life. Jimmy was brought up on the wrong side of the tracks, so to speak. He wasn't part of the country-club set, and his attitude was, "Well, I'll show those white-collar, rich people on the other side." He relished the fact that he could be irreverent. But he could only be irreverent if he was the best. If he was good, he could get away with anything. Like Ali or even McEnroe, if you're good, you get away with it. And up to that point, Connors had never been cautious. Off the ground, the only person I ever knew who hit the ball that hard was Dick Savitt. I practiced with Savitt a lot and he hit a very heavy ball. Connors also hit a heavy ball, especially off his backhand.

I tried to resist equating our final with good versus evil. But I was asked the question so often that I was forced to think about it in those terms, even though I really thought Jimmy's attitude was Bill Riordan's fault. Riordan relished his role as a manager, the way fight promoters basked in Ali's afterglow.

I know of many acts of kindness that Jimmy has bestowed on people. He loves kids. He likes giving autographs. He's done a lot of spontaneous favors for people that the media have never heard of. I definitely think that Riordan guided him the wrong way and that his mother somehow just didn't put her foot down strongly enough. So many wonderful things were happening to Jimmy at the time, yet he was being cast in the role of villain. Even when we walked into Centre Court together and made the customary bows to the Royal Box, the media noticed that I was wearing my U.S. Davis Cup warmup jacket. The fact that Jimmy had refused to play Davis Cup for the United States heightened their awareness.

But Jimmy is a fighter. He won the third set, 7–5, and led, 3–0, in the fourth. I had to decide whether or not to continue as is or blast back. I decided to continue feeding him more junk, force him to the net and lob. When I broke serve at 3–1, he became a bit tentative, which reinforced my belief that I was doing the right thing. He was human. Perhaps the pressure was getting to him.

I won five of the next six games, which must have made

174

those bettors happy who had gambled on me to win at 23 to 5 odds. When I took the match point, all the years, all the effort, all the support I had received over the years came together. My first thought and only sad moment was that Dr. Johnson had not lived to see my greatest victory. Before I walked to the net to shake hands with Jimmy, I turned to the special friends' box and held up my right fist to Donald Dell. It would be the only time in my career that I would feel such an urge.

I walked into the locker room and the first person I saw was Neale Fraser of Australia, who beat Rod Laver for the 1960 Wimbledon title. Neale stuck out his hand and said, "Welcome to the club." I realized what he meant. I was still celebrating an athletic triumph over a tough opponent, but the victory allowed me to enter a very special circle of players. Since the first Wimbledon event was played in 1877, there had been only 51 different men's champions.

Looking back, I believe my victory over Connors that day was the most significant singles match of the seventies. I fully believe that if Connors had beaten me, he would also have won the U.S. Open that fall (he lost in straight sets to Manuel Orantes of Spain) and that Bjorn Borg would not have won five straight Wimbledons. If Jimmy had won our match, he might have found a way to beat Borg, and Borg's ascendancy would have been delayed, or maybe it wouldn't have happened at all. If the time isn't right, many balloons get burst in sports. Victor Amaya led Borg two sets to one, with Borg serving at 1–3, 30–40, in the first round of the 1978 Wimbledon tournament. Borg served a fault and then a deep second serve that looked wide. If it had been a double fault, Borg would have been down 1–4, and almost out of the match.

"That linesperson was destined to call that ball in," I told Victor years later. Amazingly, Borg went for a big second serve down the middle. How could he take the risk? But he did it. Everybody thought it was a fault, but the linesman called it good, and Borg won the point on Victor's error. "You were destined to lose that match," I said. I didn't feel that way when Borg played Vijay Amritraj at Wimbledon in the early rounds of the 1979 tournament. Vijay also had Borg with his back to the wall. I was watching the match on TV that day with Jeanne and said, "Borg will win this match not because of *his* destiny, but because Vijay will choke. He will find a way to lose this match." Vijay's destiny seems to be that of a "tester" of champions.

There's a difference between intensity and killer instinct. I put killer instinct at the highest level of intensity. Boxers like Carlos Monzon and Roberto Duran have it, despite Duran's poor showing against Sugar Ray Leonard in their second fight. I even think Ali had killer instinct in the way he taunted his opponents. That bothered me a lot. I kept telling him, "Why do you have to do that? You're so good. Just box. Keep your mouth shut and just box." But he would humiliate his opponents, and that annoyed me. I don't think he had to do that. I don't like purposeful humiliation anytime.

In tennis, I think the killer instinct is a waste of energy. How do you control something like that? You work yourself into a frenzy, and you want to take advantage of every opportunity, to be opportunistic or close out, or whatever it is. I associate killer instinct with a heightened emotional state, and I would not want to be known as somebody who had it. People have said that Laver had the killer instinct. Maybe he did. In his prime, he certainly executed better than anybody else.

Cliff Richey would readily admit that he worked up a hate for his opponents. He would not talk to his opponent on the day he had to play him. Cliff made it personal. So did Richard Gonzales. To a certain extent, Connors was another one. He liked being the adversary against the crowd and his opponent. He enjoyed that role. I like harmony in everything. To me, there should be harmony among the crowd, court officials, the players, and even the ball boys—or ball persons as we call them now.

There are a lot of guys with the killer instinct who go the distance but somehow don't get anything out of it. Vijay Amritraj didn't have enough confidence to convince himself that he could beat Borg. That's why I said to Jeanne: "He will find a way to lose." But maybe people like Vijay and Jaime Fillol are better off doing what they do. You pay a price for a killer instinct. I don't care who you are, but you pay a price for that in our culture. Our economic philosophy of capitalism and our Christian ethics are complete polar opposites. We go to church on Sunday morning and are told to turn the other cheek, be a nice boy and practice everything else in the Old and New Testament. Capitalism is exactly the opposite—it's every man for himself. We're rewarded according to how much we produce and we can only "win through intimidation." Remember the Lombardi theory—look out for No. 1.

Would Jesus Christ be a quarterback if he were living today? I'm not sure what he would be. Maybe a wide receiver. Wide receivers have a certain glamour and they can take a lot of punishment too. We all pay a price for the killer instinct in some way, but it depends on individual personalities. A player has to live with himself, and not everybody is the same. John McEnroe has no trouble sleeping at night, even when some people criticize him for his behavior on the court. McEnroe has no qualms about that. Maybe he'll change as he grows older, but he seems comfortable with what he's doing now. His behavior must improve, however.

On the trip to Kitzbuhel with Vitas, we spent most of the time talking about Vitas's game. If somebody asks me about his game, I'm always willing to help. I even tried to help Wojtek Fibak with his serve, which I still think is the weakest part of his game. There aren't too many people on this earth who know more about the serve than I do. From the time I worked with Gonzales, I know how the serve works, what you have to do to hit it, place it, and avoid hitting with just your arm. I have studied the serve in great detail.

Vitas and I talked about the shots he didn't have that would help his game—a good second serve and a little bit of topspin on his backhand. And I told him that if he wanted to improve his game, he could but that he had to work on it.

I had several interesting conversations with Jimmy Connors about his game.

It will take more than killer instinct for Connors to beat Borg, but he can do it, as I told him. Currently, only two players have the potential to beat a healthy Borg regularly —Connors and McEnroe. Connors should win at least 40 percent of his matches against Borg, which he hasn't done in recent years. He can match Borg off the ground; McEnroe can't. McEnroe knows he has to come to the net eventually and win points up there to beat Borg. If McEnroe stays at the baseline, he's going to lose. Connors can match Borg shot for shot, but he should be able to do better because his approach shots could be devastating. His forehand volley needs to be changed a little bit, but there's no problem with his backhand volley. With the exception of his low forehand, Connors has very good approach shots. But if you're going to beat Borg, you have to bring him to the net. Borg rules from the service line to the back fence; he is king in that area. So, ideally, you bring Borg in with off-speed drop shots or drop volleys and lob over the two-handed backhand. That's one way to do it. Connors has some of the best passing shots the world has ever seen. But he never gets to use them because he never brings Borg in. He lobs very well and he disguises it off the backhand. But he telegraphs his forehand lob by leaning back. I've told him, "You might fool some of the young kids, but you wouldn't fool me for a second with that shot if I were playing you now. When you go over to the corner, when I start seeing you leaning back, I know you're going to throw up the lob. And I think McEnroe and Borg know that also." Nevertheless, all three of them are better than I ever was.

Jimmy could improve his serve too. His toss is absolutely awful, too far to the right for a left-handed player. He needs to be able to do more things with his serve to keep Borg off-balance.

The significance of my Wimbledon victory began to dawn on me forty-eight hours after the match. I had to make an appearance for Catalina sportswear in Pittsburgh, and fifteen hundred fans mobbed the store. My standing had changed in a permanent way, even more than after my 1968 U.S. Open victory.

Many performers in sports have never reached their potential. I believe I'm one. Neither have Ilie Nastase and Roscoe Tanner. Stan Smith did. But my win at Wimbledon was an important milestone. It marked the achievement of superior performance at least once. I had never won the French, Italian, or German titles, the big three of European clay courts, but I had captured the two most important titles in the eyes of Americans: the U.S. Open and Wimbledon.

Wimbledon is "The Championship." The winner actually gets three trophies. The most important is the All-England Tennis Club Trophy bearing the words: "Single-handed Championship of the World." I always wonder, in reading those words, if a two-handed player can enter legally. The second trophy is the Renshaw Cup given in honor of the Renshaw Brothers, and the third is the President's Cup, presented to the winner of the All-Comers Singles Championship of the World.

All that tradition, history, and pomp make these trophies very dear to me. It's a long way from Brook Field to

Wimbledon's Centre Court. They mean a lot because Wimbledon represents the highest achievement in my craft. I reached the pinnacle of an effort that began with Ron Charity in 1950 on a playground in Richmond. I was grateful and elated.

But if tradition and ceremony marked my entrance into a very exclusive club, the victory had its impact on a much more materialistic level. Like many other athletes, I had clauses in my contracts that provided for extra compensation if I reached the semifinals or finals of important events, including Wimbledon. My exhibition fees almost doubled, which meant I could make the same money in half the time. Of course, I was never a big exhibition player. I chose certain tours—Southeast Asia, Africa, and France—for the experience. But my financial value and my ability to generate income—which was my role as a professional athlete—had been upgraded considerably by my Wimbledon win.

So was my value as a speaker and as a symbol, especially for black children. But after Wimbledon, I had to learn to say no more. Bill Cosby once told me, "Some of these brothers and sisters out there will lay you out for not coming. Sammy Davis, Jr., does too many [appearances]; he's killing himself." You've got to spread yourself among family, work, and charity and you have to find a happy balance.

Sure enough, there was hostility if I turned down invitations. "How can you deny black children the opportunity to see the only heroes they really identify with?" When people said things like that I almost wished I had not won Wimbledon. But I had to weigh the good against the bad and the thrill of victory was too strong for me to feel guilty more than a few minutes.

11

Jeanne

My father looked stunned. For an instant, I thought he would faint as Jeanne Marie Moutoussamy walked through the front door of his house in Gum Springs, Virginia. He just stood there and stared at Jeanne. I had never seen him so stunned.

"What's the matter, Daddy?" I asked, after introducing him to Jeanne. She was the first woman I had ever brought to Daddy's house. As I watched him stare at Jeanne, I wondered whether he had spotted a flaw that I somehow missed since we began seeing each other months earlier.

"She looks just like your mother," he whispered, as Jeanne marveled at the house that Daddy had built. "Just like your mother."

Later that day, I looked again at an old photograph of my mother, taken when I was just four years old. Indeed, there was a strong resemblance: the straight brown hair, the high cheekbones, the large eyes, the light brown complexion. I hadn't noticed. But what haunted my father went beyond the similarity in the photograph. He kept staring at Jeanne when he thought I wasn't looking—long, hopeful glances that must have taken him back to the time before that fateful trip to the hospital. I sensed that somehow, my mother had managed to reach from beyond and influence my choice of the woman who would share my life.

I always felt I would "know" I had found THE ONE when I saw her. I saw Jeanne for the first time October 14, 1976, at the United Negro College Fund benefit at the Felt Forum in New York. She was taking my photograph. Wearing jeans, a plain beige sweater, and very little

makeup, she stood out in the cluster of professional photographers. She didn't need makeup. I thought she was
extraordinarily beautiful.

"Photographers are getting cuter these days," I said.

"Well, thank you," she replied, with a tone that told me
she wasn't impressed with my originality. She promptly
stepped on my foot as the photographers jostled for position.

I saw her again later that day and asked her name.
"Jeanne" I understood. The last name escaped me. She
spelled it out: "Moutoussamy." I repeated it to myself several times. She was with a mutual friend of ours. Later, in
the men's locker room, I asked my friend, "Is that *your*
lady with you?"

"No!" he said in a very emphatic way. That's all I wanted
to know.

After the tournament, I had an opportunity to chat with
Jeanne at the UNCF party. I was impressed by her smarts.
Her looks were obvious. I asked about dinner "at some
future date."

"When?"

"How about tomorrow?"

"OK."

We met at Thursday's for our first date and it was an
enjoyable evening. I always liked conversation and Jeanne
more than held her own. She had strong opinions, and
while we didn't agree about everything, we could argue
well into the night and stay friends.

Because I was never in any one place too long, I had
developed an approach to women based on that kind of
time frame. I sized up someone quickly if I was interested
at all. But I thought nothing of possibly blowing a date on
a marginal woman, someone I thought might be interesting or who had something to say. I had nothing to lose. I
formed lots of friendships in this way and didn't feel sex-
ually pressured. I had become a quick study of human

nature; sometimes, of course, I was wrong. There was something about Jeanne I liked.

The day after our first date, I asked her to accompany me to a benefit I was doing for my Uncle E. J. Cunningham's club in New Jersey. To my surprise, she agreed. Later, I told my Aunt Marie privately, "I think this is the one." I didn't say anything to Jeanne.

The next day, I asked if she would go with me to the World Series. She said "No." She learned quickly about my travel schedule. On the day of our first date, I had flown to St. Louis that morning for another American Airlines clinic and flown back in time to meet her. Several days later, I was headed for Europe. "I'll call you," I said. "Is that OK?"

"Sure, you can call me," she said. But I could tell from her voice that she really didn't expect me to call.

I kissed her on the cheek in the lobby of 30 Rockefeller Plaza (she worked for NBC at the time) and was off. I called from the airport and from Vienna. I called every day from Europe and talked to her on election night as Jimmy Carter went over the top. By the time I got back, we were in love; at least I was.

Marriage and the idea of marriage were always rather frightening to me. What bothered me was not so much marriage but divorce. It seems that at one end there is marriage and at the other end there is widowerhood or divorce. I thought people in general got married for the wrong reasons and turned to divorce not because they couldn't get along but because they didn't try hard enough.

As a carefree bachelor traveling all the time, I often thought about marriage and, invariably, divorce. Keeping my promise to myself to stay single until I was thirty was easy enough. I had plenty to do and there was much about life I wanted to enjoy. When I reached thirty, I literally started to look for a wife. I was ready to open up—to share my life with someone. Before then, I would have resented the restraints, not with respect to other women but restraints on my time. This may seen to be a cold-blooded approach to marriage, but I wanted to take a logical and rational view of the institution and to make sure it would work for me. Neither my father nor mother nor any aunt or uncle was divorced.

My friendships with a variety of women helped me form a healthy respect for all women. The early death of my mother prevented me from forming an ideal image the way that other men do. But over the years, I developed my own particular taste in women.

I had also evolved my own particular kind of relationship with them. Since I was always on the run, I kept in touch by telephone. I saw them when I could and was pretty much in control of the relationship. A typical example was the WCT event in Hawaii for the Avis Challenge Cup—one of those winner-take-all tournaments. In a land of beautiful women, this girl was noticeable. A beauty contest winner, she worked for Hawaiian Airlines, and was a hostess at the tournament. But what she loved most was sailing.

Our matches were scheduled at 8:30 A.M. for broadcast back to the mainland. By 10:30 one morning, I had beaten Raul Ramirez and had the rest of the day open. I had seen her from a distance, so I wrangled an introduction from a friend. I was immediately taken with her.

She was gorgeous, bright, of Japanese and Hawaiian ancestry, and a graduate of Kamehameha High School, which required Hawaiian ancestry for admission. We spent an entire day touring Kona, a stunning island of lava beaches and rocky coasts. Her explanation of events in Hawaii's history couldn't have been better if James Michener had been along.

Because of the peculiar nature of the tournament, I had to come back a week later for the semifinal phase of the winner-take-all format. The prize was now $50,000, and my opponent was Ken Rosewall. By this time, she and I had talked on the telephone every day. When I came back, I beat Rosewall and spent all my time with her.

I came back to Hawaii a third time for the final against Ilie Nastase. I lost the match. On the way to the airport in her Volkswagen, we had stopped at a red light. As the light turned green, we went into the intersection, but a car came barreling from the right. She veered left to avoid the collision. I sensed the crash coming, pulled my knees up to my chest and my arms around my head to cover my eyes.

The other car hit our right front fender at about thirty miles an hour and slammed the Volkswagen ninety degrees to the left—but we didn't turn over. I sat stunned, realized I only had superficial cuts and got out of the car, and ran around to her side. Her face and thick brown hair were red with blood, but she didn't seem seriously injured. She got out of the car under her own power—a sign that nothing was broken.

As the teenage passengers stepped out of the other car, something snapped inside. I lost my self-control. "What the hell are you doing?" I screamed. "This intersection is eight lanes wide! How did you think you could make it across on a red light? That's why your insurance is so high! You could have killed us!" Through my rage, I could tell they were very upset. They knew they were at fault.

She spent three hours having glass picked out of her face and head at the hospital. Luckily, none of the scratches were deep and the doctors assured her that her face would show no evidence of the accident. My outburst that day would remain with me. Anyone who associates me with control would have been shocked, and no one understands this side of me better than Jeanne.

For a long time, we discussed my attitude of self-control and how it has shaped my life. You really can't rationalize very much at age six. I became personally acquainted with death at that age when my grandfather died, then less than a year later the most important person in my life died and I couldn't intellectually rationalize it. My psyche had to deal with it in a very primitive way. Only an analyst or psychologist could explain it; so my curiosity got the best of me, and I decided to talk to an analyst—specifically about what effect my mother's death had on me.

A lot of people think of me as detached, aloof, cold. I am detached somewhat, and maybe a little aloof, but I'm not cold. I have a lot of empathy for life in general, for the underdog, for people in embarrassing situations. I probably withdrew in certain ways to defend myself against the negative manifestations of having lost a mother at age six. Withdrawal helps defend you, so the analyst suggested. You can build a little wall around yourself so that you let only very few things in.

Seeing adults in uncontrollable situations as a child frightened me. I saw my Aunt Lola out of control at my grandfather's funeral. Then I saw my father crying after my mother's death. I also went to church with my paternal grandmother for those religious revival-type services. I would see some sisters get the spirit, going bananas during the service. At an early age, that was frightening to me. This was even before my grandfather's death, and the sight of these people scared me into controlling my emotions.

My father also may have been scared. He became overprotective of my brother and me. He didn't want to lose anybody else. I don't know whether he tried to inhibit this fear, but I brought away negative feelings from my grandfather's funeral, seeing my aunt out of control. Not that I held any bad feeling against her, but what affected me deeply was seeing her out of control at that moment in time.

The shock of my mother's death was even more frightening. It happened very early in the morning. It was like being aroused out of a deep sleep. I woke up and all of a sudden people were crying and screaming. There might have been a different long-term reaction if it had happened at four in the afternoon. But six in the morning: it was the first thing I remembered. In fact, I don't remember waking up. I just remember being put on Daddy's knee, wiping the sleep from my eyes, and my father crying like hell.

My mother's death was very frustrating. I looked at the numbers and got angry. I've always been fascinated by numbers. For instance, the chances are about one in ten that some kid born in America will be black. I fit into that one-in-ten category. Chances are one in a billion that some black kid from the South would someday grow up and win Wimbledon. But again they're one in ten that my mother would be the one to die first, among all the other aunts and uncles. And what were the chances of me, Arthur Ashe, a professional athlete, having a heart attack at thirty-seven? Yet it happened.

I'm positive my mother's death made it easier for me not to become entangled with anybody in my twenties. After Pat Battles and I broke up our engagement, I sort of said to myself, "OK, I'm not going to get married until I'm thirty." I didn't say it to anybody else, but it was in my mind.

I lived with and traveled the world with another woman for most of a year. She was a beautiful blonde Jewish Canadian woman who was an artist for a large department store. She was the first blonde I had ever been out with and the first Jewish girl I had dated since UCLA. Her family was not pleased about our relationship at first and her brother-in-law told her initially that I was not to set foot in his house. But she stood her ground, and I was amazed. She endured and eventually conquered. I was even accepted by her parents. We had dinner together— and they paid.

I never pressed my father about his feelings toward the

women I dated. After I left home at eighteen, he never interfered with my private life. I don't think it would have bothered him no matter whom I married. Our family was the product of mixed liaisons (legal and illegal), and there were quite a few interracial marriages in our family.

Marriage was always in my plans, even if it frightened me. I was not one of those guys who went around saying, "I'm a confirmed bachelor," like the caricatures in the movies or the *New Yorker*. If I was going to give myself a chance to live out the dreams that I had when I was a kid reading all those *National Geographic*s I couldn't get married. And it worried me that I might have to do things that I just didn't want to do at the time. Women like you to open up, emotionally. They want you to be vulnerable. It's natural for a six-year-old to cling to his mother or father. A heart attack leaves you vulnerable psychologically, as far as death is concerned. But it has nothing to do with the emotions of dealing with people. I can't play tennis anymore or run a ten-kilometer road race. But there's a difference between this vulnerability and the survival you face as a child. A pimp or petty thief survive differently than Mr. Thalhimer did as a Jew in Richmond.

Jeanne was the first person who sensed that I may have closed off emotional relationships with women because of the death of my mother. My brother, my father, and I slept in the same room for five years, before my father remarried. At that stage of my life, I developed bonds of closeness that stayed there for a long time. It explains why my brother and I feel overly protective of my father now. Neither of us would ever let anything happen to him, if we can help it. And my stepmother is a very good God-fearing woman. Jeanne thinks the fear of losing my father and the recurrence of the great pain associated with loss of my mother contribute to my fixations on death. She also believes that some of my internalizing is a form of denial.

Jeanne

"You'll often deny things you feel physically or spiritually," she once said. "For fear of the emotions and response related to it."

Jeanne captivated me. In looks, she was easily a "10," but she did something else to me. She was a photographer and graphic artist who was bright, articulate, sensitive. Even with all my traveling in late 1976, to Europe and Australia, I knew I wanted to marry Jeanne. It was intuition mingled with being able to recognize genuine feelings for someone.

Jeanne came from a mix of ancestries that included blacks and East Indians. Her grandfather was born in India. Her original family name was Moutouswammy. She was from Chicago, had attended prestigious Cooper Union, and had lived in New York for six years and was independent. Her independence became a source of positive and negative influences in our relationship.

When I made the decision to get married, it was a very serious step for me. I tried not to look at it cold-bloodedly, but I had to think logically: "Will it work?" Aside from the fact that I love this person, will it work? Are we compatible? Do our personalities mesh? I can't just be swept away completely in the emotion of the moment or the time. That's why not enough marriages last.

I didn't force a relationship on Jeanne trying to overlook the bad points and glorify the good. We had to put everything together and decide whether we could be compatible.

We reinforced our relationship through extensive conversations. Jeanne always wanted to know how I decided that she was the one. "With all of the bright, independent women that you met over the years," she would say, "why me?"

People either stand the test of time or they don't. You can't always come up with reasons why something didn't work out. Either it did or it didn't. Why did so-and-so get

189

divorced? Why didn't Farrah Fawcett and Lee Majors stay together?

Initially, I had a big hunch about Jeanne that sprang from emotion. I met her, I liked her, it turned into love. After a while, I unconsciously started comparing this person with previous relationships. I did it unconsciously; everybody does. If it stands the test of time, you've got something. If it doesn't, bad luck, but you haven't lost anything.

Jeanne always said she was excited about our relationship though she had never dated anyone who had traveled quite as much. "And I've never had a relationship over the telephone either," she would tell me. "Especially somebody calling me every day from Europe and Australia." I think she felt that it must have been serious if I called from Australia. When she invited me to come home and meet her family on Thanksgiving, I knew she must have felt good about us.

"Do you know the first thing my aunts asked me that day?" she would recall years later, about our visit to Chicago. "They said, 'Has Arthur asked you to marry him yet?' "

"What did you tell them?"

"I said, 'No, God, I've only known him a month!' "

Jeanne had some preconceived notions about me. In the beginning, these notions are unavoidable, even if they are a bit unfair. If someone were to begin a relationship with Ronald Reagan, they would already know quite a bit about him from all the publicity. But Ronald Reagan doesn't know them, so he's at a disadvantage. I was an athlete. A black athlete. Black women treated me differently because they knew something about me and some immediately tried to make me feel that I wasn't really the great person they thought I thought I was.

Jeanne never felt that way. But ask any black man who is just recently married about his relationships with black women, and he'll tell you that black women are tough initially. The reason is because they have been disappointed so often. They are understandably very wary.

Jeanne says that 95 percent of the black men she dated had some sort of "line" and that a lot of black women fall for it. She's right. I've heard some of the lines my friends have used—how beautiful some women are, how much these guys want to wine and dine them, how much ambition the guys have.

"But all of a sudden, it's all gone," Jeanne would say, when we discussed the subject. "It's not there. The feelings are not there, the ambition is not there, it changes and there is something false, very false about the relationship."

Black men seem to feel more of a compulsion to dominate black women than white men feel about dominating their women. There appears to be a basic insecurity. The black male feels he is not always the equal of the white male because he may not have as much power as the president of General Motors and may never have it. So he has his own little circle of friends, and his woman has to deal with all the grief and disappointment. And the double standard works much more viciously in black America than it does in white America. The black man will say, "Well, I can fool around, but my woman better not fool around." He wants to dominate somebody—like all men. But the insecurity of the black woman comes from the fact that she has been disappointed so damn many times by black men who feed her a line and flatter the hell out of her.

Until recently, black men have had few outlets for their egos. One way was to try to conquer as many women as they could. So some black men have become pimps; others are preachers of the storefront church where they are the big fish in the little pond. But now, fortunately, black middle America is growing and prospering like never before.

Jeanne felt that the ego of black men was under enormous stress because so many black women were getting better jobs than black men. "If you see a black male who's a blue-collar worker walking down the street," she would tell me, "and you're a sister in a two-piece suit and attaché case, if they whistle at you or tell you that you look nice and you don't reciprocate by smiling, saying thank you, or looking at them eye-to-eye, they'll curse you out."

That's part of the rules of being black. No matter who you are, we black people are supposed to say hello to one another, even if they have never seen that person before. If you are black, you say hello back.

Jeanne thought I was different because she had read about me and seen me on several talk shows. But she was also expecting some kind of line based on her previous experiences with black men, so I was consciously more distant with her when we started dating. No kissing, no holding hands, not even privately.

On our first date, I was sitting on a little stone block, reading a book in the foyer at NBC waiting for her. She came down the stairs and said, "How was your trip?" I said, "fine," and then handed her a red rose, which pleasantly caught her completely by surprise.

As Jeanne learned about my family, she said the rose touched her even more because they were my mother's favorite flower.

I even surprised Jeanne with the engagement ring. I didn't formally propose. Instead, I put the wedding ring in an envelope in her medicine cabinet. It took her three days to find the envelope.

My travel trimmed considerably that winter. I went to Australia, but problems with my heel affected my play and forced me to shorten the trip. I returned home and made two decisions: I would have heel surgery and get married.

I had surgery on my foot to remove bone chips on February 10, 1977. On February 20, Jeanne and I were married by Rev. Andrew Young, then the UN ambassador.

Jeanne

I had met Andy in 1974 at the *Washington Star* tournament. I was chatting when I noticed him on the other side of a wooden fence separating us. I waved and went over to speak to him. He had always been someone I idolized. We got into a conversation and met several times afterward to talk. I attended his swearing-in at the White House and asked him after the ceremony if he would perform the marriage. He said yes immediately.

The night before Jeanne and I were married, Andy and his wife, Jean, invited us to dinner in their suite at the Waldorf Towers. They talked about the sanctity of marriage. Jean Young said they felt responsible for all the couples that Andy married. It was clear that Jean would be as much a part of the ceremony as Jeanne and it made us feel better that they would always be "on call" if there were trouble.

"When a couple marries," Andy said, "six people are really involved. There are two people—yes, but they are different people at different times. First, there is the person you are. Then there is the person you think you are and then finally there is the person others think you are. Most of the time, these three people are not the same."

"The trick," Jean Young went on, "is to know which person you are at any one time. There will be many times when you'll want to grit your teeth and quit. You have to resist that. Forgiveness will seem mighty difficult, but no marriage can survive without that."

Andy and Jean were right. I constantly try to figure out which person I am. Confusing these roles can bring trouble, especially for someone in the public eye. I am not the person people think I am. I can put on a mask on some occasions and be what I have to be until my work is finished. I am asked often how I developed so much patience. I'm patient only as long as I have to be. After hours, I can be as impatient as anybody else.

Fans of athletes, politicians, and entertainers admire an

image, not the person. That third person Andy mentioned, "the person people think you are," can get you in the most trouble because the public's thinking can change. I have kept that conversation with the Youngs in the forefront of my mind ever since.

The early days of our marriage tested some of these images. Since I didn't have a well-defined sense of what my wife should be like, no matter how deliberate I had tried to be or how much I tried to idealize our relationship, it was not what I thought it would be. That happens to everybody, so I gathered.

One of our first problems involved Jeanne's independence. She felt uncomfortable with me trying to do things for her career; she wanted to do things on her own, not as Mrs. Arthur Ashe. She realized that I could pull a string here and there to help her career along a little faster. But she did not want her contemporaries in photography to feel that she had gotten this assistance without merit.

In the beginning, I don't think I understood what Jeanne was feeling. Later, she would tell me that she didn't explain it in a way that I could understand. Emotions prevailed over logic, and I went to the other extreme: I decided I wouldn't help Jeanne at all. "If you want something done," I finally told her, "don't ask me. I'm not going to make a phone call or write a letter. I won't do anything." But even my withdrawal could not hide the fact that she was still "Arthur Ashe's wife," and the public would not know that I wasn't helping her.

It was very frustrating for both of us. She would walk into a photo editor's office with her portfolio, come out ten minutes later, and the phone editor might have asked "How is your husband doing? I met him once at a sports exhibition. Tell him I said hello." She would say, "Well, what did you think of the portfolio?" The editor would say, "Oh, yeah, it's nice, but we can't use it now." Jeanne began to feel that the associations she had with some editors came about because they wanted to get close to me and not because they were interested in her work.

"You have to be a very secure, mature person to handle that properly," she said. "At twenty-five, and not being fully established and totally secure in my work, that was very difficult for me to deal with. And I had gone from making $22,000 a year at NBC to absolutely nothing. I had quit my job and become a wife, and it was traumatic."

The problems involved more than pictures. Jeanne liked her last name. She was proud of it, and she didn't want to change her name. I didn't put up any fuss about it. "Fine," I said. "Don't change your name." But at social functions or tennis matches, people would still come up and say, "Oh, hello, Mrs. Ashe," and Jeanne would do a slow burn. She didn't like being known as Mrs. Arthur Ashe. And then she developed a sort of priority list over the names that she hated the most. At the top was "Mrs. Arthur Ashe." Then came "Mrs. Jeanne Ashe." After that was "Mrs. Jeanne Moutoussamy-Ashe." At the bottom was "Jeanne Moutoussamy." She'd been called that for one-quarter of a century.

On a deeper level, it wasn't just a sense of being called "Mrs. Arthur Ashe." Some of the other women I dated would have loved the idea. But Jeanne liked the person she was before she began dating me, and nobody could see that because she was overshadowed by me. The fact that my father, brother, and I are very strong figures— no-nonsense types—made it all the more difficult. My father had no idea there were any problems. If he had suspected it, he probably would have told Jeanne, "Hey, if you don't like the name, leave." My father is like that, plain and simple. From the context of his world, a woman marries a man and takes his name. Everybody in his family had done it; that was his total experience.

Jeanne and I worked out the difficulties. Time and the security of our relationship helped. Her own recognition of who she is in the roles that she plays and her security in her own work contributed. She is a good photographer who had developed her own ideas about her work without preconceptions about what she wanted to do. In the first few years she may have used me as a yardstick for success because everyone was constantly looking to me for approval. If people look at you for approval, you become a symbol of power. Jeanne was caught up in that sense of power and success.

The difference between how people treated Jeanne when she was alone or with me was day and night. It affected her ego and confused her until she was able to sort out the areas she wanted to go into and how she would go about doing it. If people don't like her work now, bad luck. She's satisfied with where it's going and what she's doing. She doesn't work as much as she feels she should, but that's only a matter of her getting out, not worrying about my role.

The pluses of being with Jeanne overshadowed that early period of adjustment. I get along very well with her family, especially her father. We have become very good friends, and we're similar in lots of ways. We like to play golf, are temperamentally alike, and both of us have gone through heart attacks. I hear jokes all the time about not getting along with in-laws, but that wasn't the case with me, and it's a big plus to a relationship. So were the interesting people I met through Jeanne. As an artist, she was well connected in the New York community, black and white. I was interested in art, and it had always fascinated me, but I didn't know much about it until I met Jeanne and her friends.

Romare Bearden, for example, is the most famous living black artist. He had known Jeanne for years. Meeting him and talking with him was a treat. Jeanne invited James VanDerzee over for dinner one night, several years ago. His parents were the maid and butler for President Ulysses S. Grant. He's ninety-four years old and was the first great black photographer; he got his first camera through selling seeds in the mail-order business. I took pictures of Jeanne and Mr. VanDerzee sitting around the apartment that night. They were talking about what it was like photographing Harlem in the 1930s. Before I met Jeanne, she always spent Mr. VanDerzee's birthday with him. Even when I had been in Australia before we were married, she spent New Year's Eve with him. Jeanne feels very close to Mr. VanDerzee; after his wife died, she helped with the funeral arrangements.

Howard Cosell likes to tease me about the fact that I married above myself. He will see Jeanne, walk up and tell her, as only Cosell can, "Jeanne, I don't know why you married beneath yourself." Howard was a bigger hit at our wedding reception than Jeanne and I were.

I never felt marriage would be smooth sailing, but I never thought we would have problems in the areas that we did. I read somewhere that the two biggest reasons for divorce are sex and money. I remember reading an article in *U.S. News & World Report* about a guy who had voted for Ronald Reagan in the 1980 presidential election. The guy knew his salary was not going to go up until the dollar got stronger. When he was asked about his relationship with his wife, he replied, "Oh, it's all right." The interviewer then asked what he and his wife had argued about the most. "Money," he said.

Jeanne and I had no problems with sex or money. The difference between our relationship and others was who I was. I felt it was because of my name, but Jeanne felt it was because of an unusual situation. She wasn't looking for a red carpet. From my standpoint, it was not a red carpet. My tennis career was winding up anyway. I could feel it.

The first sign came in 1976 when Harold Solomon beat me in the WCT finals in Dallas. When you're thirty-three years old and a professional athlete, the possibility that your career will end always lurks in the back of your mind. I would not admit it then, but that loss marked the beginning of the end. It was a signal, which I tried hard to ignore, that I had passed my peak as an athlete. At Wimbledon that summer, the year after I had beaten Jimmy Connors, I lost to Vitas Gerulaitis in the round of sixteen. Vitas was simply younger and faster; I could smell something happening, and I had to work hard not to panic.

Injuries are another sign of battle fatigue. I reinjured my foot in practice and decided to take the rest of 1977 off. Time was slipping away, and I didn't want to end my career on a bad foot, but the physical problems began to pile up anyway. I developed iritis, an inflammation of the iris, which was extremely painful.

I tried to make use of my free time with workouts on the Nautilus machines at the Sports Training Institute. But when you're trying to make a comeback after a long layoff, a professional athlete in his thirties is full of self-doubt. I had undergone surgery, come back, hurt my heel again, and worked hard to get into the best physical shape I could. But I was not sure of the effects of my experiences in the last year.

About the same time, something else happened which affected my outlook. Catalina, the apparel company I had been with for eight years, decided I was no longer worth the royalty they had been paying me. I was terribly hurt by their decision. I never thought a company would want to dump me for what I thought was the wrong reason. I had helped them build their image in tennis; now that I was no longer at the very top they seemed to have little use for me. I had been loyal and believed that players who switched companies all the time shortchanged themselves and their employers, but I had no choice. Donald Dell and I strongly believed that I should get a royalty if my name was on any product; I was being forced out at a time when I was struggling to regain my place in the tennis world. I felt I had been betrayed and promised myself that I would not be so vulnerable again. Of course, from their stand-point, they just had to make a hard-nosed business deci-sion. We parted on friendly terms.

During these upheavals, I kept thinking I had to hasten my readiness for retirement. I worried less about my ten-nis results and more about my business involvements. Meetings that once had been a nuisance now took on new importance. I began an instructional four-color series for *Tennis Magazine.* I made commercials for the National Guard. I went to work for Aetna Life and Casualty as a consultant.

My tennis results in 1978 were inconsistent. I won a $50,000 event in San Jose, California, beating Gene Mayer and Bernie Mitton. The win did wonders for my confi-dence and convinced me I could still play. Three months later, I beat Bob Lutz in the finals of a $75,000 event in Columbus and then won what was to be my last tourna-ment title, over Brian Gottfried, at the Pacific Southwest championships. Fittingly, the victory came in Los Angeles, the city where I reached my maturity as a player.

The win put me within striking distance of the top eight players who would qualify for the Grand Prix Masters tournament at Madison Square Garden. I had qualified for the eight-player season-ending events before, but this one took on new importance for me. I had a feeling it would be my last chance to win the Masters.

My contract with Doral required that I be in Florida during the Christmas holidays. I asked Al Schragis and Howard Kaskel to let me go to Australia one last time to see if I could get the points I needed. They were under-standing and agreed. Before leaving for Australia, how-ever, I had to go to Sweden for Davis Cup matches. Vitas and I were the singles players, Smith and Lutz were the doubles team. I lost to Borg, but beat Kjell Johansson, and we won the series, 3–2. In my last Davis Cup event, I set an American record for singles victories—27.

I then flew thirty-four hours to Australia, via Stockholm, Zurich, Bahrain, Singapore, Sydney, and Brisbane. I arrived on a Wednesday morning and played my first match at 5:30 that evening. Miraculously, I reached the semifinals and won enough points to put me in the Masters; but time was running out.

It would have been a fairy tale if I somehow had managed to win the 1979 Masters. For a while, the dice seemed to be rolling in my favor. I beat Gottfried and Solomon, and Connors defaulted to me because of an injury. I had two match points on McEnroe in the final; but like the fighter he is, McEnroe fought back and won in three sets.

I feel lucky to be alive. My physical condition may have been the difference. A disproportionately high percentage of thirty- to forty-five-year-olds die from first heart attacks. Older men have a higher survival rate from first heart attacks because they develop what is called collateral circulation, alternate routes for blood to travel when an artery is blocked. Apparently, my training for tennis accelerated this development.

Many people wonder how someone who never smoked, was not overweight, did not eat fatty foods, and was in great physical shape could have a heart attack. Family history and stress were the chief factors in my case. Both sides of my family suffer from hypertension and heart disease. Because tendencies toward heart trouble are more prevalent in males, Jeanne and I have reason to worry. Both our fathers have heart trouble, so we hope our children will be girls. While I would love to have a son, I worry about the possible consequences. We have even talked about not having children at all.

It was fun to be on top. I was treated royally. What I said got the attention of the media. My name was bandied about the gossip columns. But you pay a premium for privacy.

The events of August 1, 1979, changed my life in ways I could not imagine. I have long scars on my lower legs to mark the long line where veins were removed and used in my coronary-bypass operation. I have had to think about death, and this has made life more precious. When I get a pain in my chest—any pain—I wonder if something is wrong. I never get used to the tics and twinges. I keep hoping I'll develop some internal system to sort the ordinary chest pains from heart trouble.

If you casually watch TV or read magazines, you can't help but become at least superficially familiar with the warning signs of the major diseases like cancer and heart attacks. When I went into New York Hospital that August afternoon, there was a possibility that I could die. My task was to grab myself by the shoulders and say, "From this day forward, your life is going to be different."

But in philosophical terms, it shattered a myth that every professional athlete has about invincibility. Athletes, especially those involved in aerobic sports, are in great shape. If they catch cold or sneeze, they consider it a personal affront. Society believes that if you lead the National Football League in pass receptions, you're not supposed to get sick. And when you do get sick, it brings you back to life, back to reality.

One day I remember walking home from New York Hospital after a checkup with Dr. Mike Collins and Dr. Virginia Bouchard Smith. I had just been catheterized, and they saw the results. They showed much more damage than was originally thought, a lot more than my symptoms showed. From the results of my cath, I should have had more pain than I had and my heart attack should have been more severe. They just said point-blank to me that day, "You can never play tennis again unless you have an operation." That was the first time I ever thought about having open heart surgery.

If the open heart surgery were successful, they thought it was possible that I could come back and play tennis, although they didn't know anybody who had done it.

Two months later, after watching *Monday Night Football*

Arthur Ashe: OFF THE COURT

in Jacksonville, Florida, I started getting palpitations. Palpitations are nothing more than a subjective sense of a heart beat. But it scared me because I knew my arteries were clogged. So the next morning, Charlie Pasarell took me to Jacksonville Memorial Hospital. After two days of tests, they told me nothing was wrong, but I still didn't know what to expect. While in the hospital, I met a guy who had just undergone a triple bypass two days before. He was in great shape: no blood, one tube in his arm, no oxygen, all he had was a simple dressing. He said all the pain was gone, and that he wasn't even on medication anymore. So I went back home and resolved that I would get this done myself.

There are three places that are famous for these operations—the Cleveland Clinic, the Baylor Medical Center, and New York. I just happened to have a fraternity brother, Dr. John Hutchinson, a black surgeon, who did them for a living. I called him up and told his secretary that I would take his first opening.

"He won't have anything for a couple of weeks," she said. I said I would take the first opening whenever it was. That was on a Saturday. She called back in two hours and said "We can do you on Thursday morning. Check into the hospital Monday no later than 3 P.M."

I didn't want to live as if I were walking around on eggshells. It sort of hit me one day when I went to pick up a pair of glasses at Sixty-fifth Street and Third Avenue. While walking from there to the hospital seven blocks away, I started getting chest pains from walking too fast down the street. I was just walking and I thought to myself, "Well, look I know what this operation is like, but I'll risk it. I don't want to live like this."

Jeanne understood what I was going through. She saw me lying on the table in New York Hospital that August day and knew that she had to assume control of the situation. She was frightened for me but also sensed that I was most comfortable in a calm, controlled environment. If I read panic in her eyes, she reasoned, it would not help my attitude.

I've come to depend on Jeanne for certain things that I may have taken for granted previously. It's comforting to know that you don't have to go through some crisis all by yourself. It was even more comforting in a sense that she knew what to expect because she had been through it before with her father.

Any notion I had about returning to tennis after my bypass surgery was dashed on March 9, 1980. I was in Cairo with Jeanne and Doug Stein. The trip was part business and pleasure, and we had toured the Cairo Museum, the Sphinx, and the Pyramids.

In the afternoon, after lunch at the Nile Hilton, I decided to go out for a run. A hundred yards into my jog, I felt a twinge of angina. I was scared stiff, 5,000 miles from New York Hospital, and the fear of another heart attack in Cairo loomed large. But Doug was there. He had me do some jumping jacks in my room, and the pain came back again. My playing days were over.

I constantly live with the possibility of chest pain from physical exertion. I am still adjusting to a life of limited physical activity. It's as if Cheops and King Tut put the hex on me for trespassing on their sacred burial ground. The physical adjustment has been easier than the psychological one. The change from professional to weekend player has not been as difficult as the change from uninhibited physical activity to careful consideration of any physical exertion.

Whenever I want to do something requiring a great deal of exertion, I must start slowly and take a nitroglycerin tablet. The possibility of another heart attack is always on the edge of my consciousness. Not that I expect one. Many people have heart attacks in their thirties and live to be ninety. But I haven't had enough time to get used to my new physical status. Ironically, I'm in good health in every other physical respect. I've never even had a cavity. I never had a headache until I started taking nitro in the hospital.

When I played tennis, I loved the idea of waking up, feeling nervous about the consequences of winning or losing, enjoying the pressures of staying on top. My life has been turned around. I am an ex-player. I attend the important tournaments. I captain the U.S. Davis Cup team. But I can only pick up a tennis racquet for fun. Jeanne still complains that I try to do too much. But now I'm trying new things.

Then, Now, Hereafter

I feel this is a good time to offer some observations about trends and practices that I feel strongly about.

Tennis is a metaphor for life. Many aspects of the game can be translated into life experiences; the traits needed for success in tennis are useful in other circumstances. When I was learning the game, Bobby Johnson admonished me to hit through the ball. Contact with the ball at the critical moment was an important consideration, but it was only a small part of a total concept. I couldn't strike the ball well if I didn't think in terms of the complete swing.

That insight into the nature of the tennis stroke enabled me to hit my backhand as fast and hard as I did. I've had players say to me, "You hit a backhand that was the hardest I've ever seen." I welcomed the compliment—not only for what it did for my ego—but as proof of the correctness of my tennis form.

My concentration on the mechanics of style were not limited to action on the tennis court. The notion of following through has always been important to me. In my family, it translated into "finish what you start." I had to finish all the food on my plate, not just the rice, which I liked best. When I wanted to learn to swim, I had to take all the lessons. When I asked my father if I could play in the junior high school band, his first question was, "Are you going to stick with it?"

In the beginning, concentration was a challenge. I learned to concentrate well as a junior player. I looked forward to the instructions I got from Dr. Johnson before a match and measured my success as much from my ability to execute his orders as from the outcome of the match.

But until I was fifteen, I was afraid to venture my own opinion about what to do against an opponent. Gradually, I learned that concentration also meant thinking about the totality of the match.

I knew what everyone on a tennis court was supposed to do during the match. I tuned in to every aspect of the game. If a ball boy was out of place, if a linesperson was positioned wrong, I knew it. I kept careful track of the score because Dr. J assumed that some of our white opponents would try to cheat us. I catalogued a long list of statistics about my opponent: How many forehand returns did he miss cross-court? Where did he go on his second serve at 15–30? Keeping track of these events required intense concentration, but they paid off in victories.

A certain single-mindedness is important to be successful. I've always thought that. Although I worked hard at my game, I was too curious for my own good. Bjorn Borg, for instance, never looks around during a match. When he is not playing a point, his head is down as if he's looking for a four-leaf clover. Some very good players can break their concentration on the court during a match: Ilie Nastase, Tom Okker, and, to some extent, Jimmy Connors do it. I let my attention wander because I always want to know what's going on in the world. Being a good tennis player was not enough. Narrowness didn't suit me.

When I speak of single-mindedness, I mean the dedication that a Borg, Laver, or Rosewall brings to their craft. They will still be good tennis players when they're eighty years old. It's no accident that they are good. They never got too involved in tennis politics or other distractions. And it paid off on the court. I understood the danger of "getting off track," but the tracks were too narrow for me.

Another aspect of life that has a parallel in tennis is *court presence*. The French have a term for it: "le droit de terre" —the homecourt advantage. Billie Jean King in her prime had it. So did John Newcombe. Borg has it. I never thought that Laver and Rosewall had court presence—maybe because they didn't flaunt it. They were so good they didn't have to. When you're up against a player with court presence, you feel you have to play your best to win. Even worse, you may feel you have no chance at all. Certain public figures exude court presence: Henry Kissinger and Lyndon Johnson, for example. Richard Nixon never did. People with court presence look you right in the eye, much like the face-off between Sugar Ray Leonard and Wilfredo Benitez before their fight.

Of course, a little power can corrupt. I've seen people take their "presence" too far. Johan Kriek, for example, once abused his privilege. During practice at a WCT event in Richmond, a black man in work clothes picked up Kriek's racquets, which were on the ground at the side of the court, and laid them carefully on the linesman's chair directly behind Kriek. He was momentarily outraged.

"I want my racquets here beside the baseline," Kriek said to the workman.

"I'm sorry," the man answered, "but you can't leave them on the court. You might have an accident."

"I'll put them where I please," Kriek replied angrily.

"Well, son," the black man drawled. "If you want to play here on this court, you'll leave your racquets on the chair where I put them." His tone was measured and unruffled.

"Who are you to tell me where I can put my racquet?" Kriek shouted.

"Who I am doesn't matter. What matters is a city ordinance governing safety in this coliseum."

After a couple of anxious minutes, Kriek relented. He didn't know I was watching the episode from an open door twenty yards away and that the man in work clothes was my father. I knew that Kriek, a South African, was not accustomed to taking orders from a black man.

Some young players may find it difficult to zero in on long-range solutions to problems. For a twenty-year-old, "long-range" is five years. For an elderly person, imminent death is the pressing problem. Young tennis players often panic if something bad happens in the first set of a match. It takes experience and a long-range view to put immediate events into perspective. The difference between a three-set match and a five-set match is like the difference between a ten-round and a fifteen-round boxing match. The athlete has to pace himself differently for each event.

Life, like sporting events, needs pacing. After reading Gail Sheehy's *Passages* and Levinson's *Seasons of a Man's Life,* I've come to the conclusion that life is, indeed, lived in stages, like the five-set tennis match. Few people see how difficult sacrifices will pay off later. The late Rafael Osuna was a master at this tactic. He would take what seemed to be foolish chances early in a match. Sometimes he got burned and sometimes he won the point. But he knew that when things got tight and tense in the late stages of the match, his opponent would only remember the spectacular shots Osuna had won at the beginning.

The ultimate connection between tennis and life is "in the doing"—not the winning. Vince Lombardi's statement "winning is not everything, it's the only thing" is taken too literally. Success is a journey, not a destination. The doing is usually more important than the outcome. Not everyone can be No. 1. What happens to the person who ends up No. 2 or No. 20?

I've played matches where the pace left me indifferent to the outcome. I enjoyed the combat and trying to out-think the other guy. Like Rod Laver. Each time we played, I tried to come up with a new strategy to beat him. It never worked. If I served wide to Rod's backhand, he would chip a low and soft return cross-court to my forehand (my weakest shot). He would position himself for a forehand (his strong shot). Losing to him was frustrating, but there were times I marveled at what Laver could do anyway.

I deliberately tried to meet people who I thought had something to say or something to contribute to mankind —in essence to find out what made them tick. My favorite readings are biographies. After the cast came off my foot from heel surgery, ABC's *Wide World of Sports* asked me to do a documentary on sport in South Africa. Jeanne and I went there with a crew from ABC and one of their producers, Terry O'Neil. We recorded the country's attempts to integrate athletics within the framework of apartheid. I interviewed Dr. Koornhof again and even went to his home. His arguments were no more convincing than they were the last time we talked.

On the way back, we stopped off at the Organization of African Unity Conference in Abidjan to interview Dr. Abraham Ordia, the OAU's minister of sports. Initially, Dr. Ordia didn't seem to understand the significance of the largest American sports network doing a feature on the subject of segregated sport in South Africa. We had to spend considerable energy pinning him down for an interview. Once we cornered him, he was very cooperative, and just as adamant as Dr. Koornhof.

"Unless South Africa changes, we shouldn't play with them," he said. We also talked to Denis Brutus, the Colored South African activist and poet. The story aired to good response on ABC and brought the issues of the 1976 Montreal Olympics boycott by black African nations into sharp focus for the American audience.

Some of my contacts with heads of state were less formal. In the fall of 1975, I went to Jamaica for Nations Cup matches and met Prime Minister Michael Manley. He invited me to Government House for a talk and explained his advocacy of the "New World Economic Order" and his efforts to make new ties for Jamaica in the Third World. I told him I understood, but warned that the United States was not likely to support his efforts. In fact, the U.S. government applied considerable pressure on Manley's government, and he eventually lost the next election to Edward Seaga in 1980.

My most harrowing experience with international politics took place in February 1976. I went to Nigeria to participate in that country's first professional tennis tournament. On Friday, February 13, the country's president, Murtala Muhammad, was assassinated in a coup. For three days, the players were holed up in the U.S. Embassy compound waiting for events to sort themselves out.

After three days, we became impatient to get out. However, we were told we would not get our money unless we completed the tournament. Finally, we persuaded government officials in charge of the event to let it continue. I was in the middle of my service motion, up one set over Jeff Borowiak and tied 1-all in the second, when a group of soldiers brandishing machine guns burst into the tennis stadium.

"What the hell is going on here?" shouted the soldier in charge. "What are you doing? You're playing games while we're mourning the death of our president." They were enraged.

The Nigerians in the stands panicked and began to flee. The Europeans moved a shade more slowly to get out. One of the soldiers stuck his machine gun in my back and shoved me off the court. I could feel the cold steel in my back through my wet shirt and there was a sinking feeling in my stomach. I waited for the weapon to go off as I scrambled from the court. Once I was off and it seemed clear I had no intention of returning, the soldier let me go and directed his attention toward some of his countrymen.

Four minutes later, we climbed into a government car to go back to the Embassy residence, but right in the middle of the road was the soldier who had shouted at me. He was mercilessly beating a Nigerian who had been trying to get away on a motorcycle. Jeff and I decided to pass up the car and head the other way on foot. One hundred yards away, a large official limousine stopped in front of us. It was the Hungarian ambassador, who had been a spectator. He recognized us and offered us rides back to the U.S. Embassy. Black Africa's first professional tennis event did not go very well.

Black unity has taken interesting paths. I read about Pan-Africanism, for instance, in the writings of W. E. B. DuBois and Kwame Nkrumah; Stokely Carmichael also spoke of it. Yet my numerous trips to and around Africa and in North and South America lead me to believe that Pan-Africanism as originally conceived is just some dream of a few black intellectuals.

Only two threads bind Africans and their descendants —our darker skins and our shared nonacceptance by the controlling white society. Those two things hardly form the basis for world-wide unity on any broad-based scale. Africa below the Sahara and north of the Limpopo River is more diverse than any comparably sized piece of real estate I can think of. A Masai in the Central Kenyan Highlands has little in common with a Yoruba in Eastern Nigeria except the color of his skin. The cultures are different; the language is different; the tribal customs are different (Ron Karenga notwithstanding); their topographical environment is different; their history is different, and they will have different futures. A Swede is more akin to a Yugoslav than a Watusi is to a Zulu. Pan-Africanism must be redefined in more realistic terms for it to be an attainable and worthwhile goal. As long as a Kenyan needs a visa to make a visit to next-door Tanzania or Zambia, we've got a long way to go toward African unity.

Adam Smith's "invisible hand" does not always operate in the black community—or the majority community either for that matter. I have maintained some of my earned resources in the black community. But the truth is that the black community, at present, doesn't provide the best "short term" return on investment. If it did, our communities in our nation's inner cities would be more economically viable. And we can't do it by ourselves. Investment in training programs for minorities would, however, pay handsomely over the "long term."

For example, I fully believe that the minimum-wage law works to the detriment of the inner city. My father, who is always attuned to the street, tells me that $3.30 an hour is keeping a lot of blacks out of work. Some people want to hire kids, black or white, but can't afford $3.30, he says. He is right. If an employer is forced to choose between hiring an unskilled fifteen-year-old for $3.30 or doing without, he'll do without.

My brother, a Marine officer, tells me, "A lot of our recruits come in here because they can't get a job on the outside, not because they want to be one of the chosen 'few good men.' " Like it or not, a two tiered minimum wage proposal is worth a try. Teenagers could use $2.50 an hour to amass a few dollars and then look for a better job to acquire the training for advancement where they are. I'm fed up with the alternative—50 percent teenage unemployment. I know all about the argument of the lower tier putting semiskilled adults out of work, but it's time to try something different.

I also favor registration for all eighteen-year-olds. I'm not in favor of the draft and would only favor it in a congressionally debated emergency. And I fully realize the dangers inherent in a more conservative Congress. However, if any emergency call-up is necessary, where do we start? The lessons of Vietnam are still clear in my mind. My brother was wounded twice, and forty-five thousand lives were lost in a war that most believe to have been unnecessary.

In my job as an Aetna consultant, I've talked to about four thousand college students from Palo Alto to Pittsburgh over the last few years. Their overwhelming sentiment about Selective Service was expressed by a student at

Springfield College in Massachusetts who told me, "I'll register when the Russians are at the mouth of the Connecticut River." That comment drew a big laugh, of course, but I didn't think it was that amusing. If we are not willing to sacrifice anything for our ideals, we'll probably lose them.

Coming from a black man, that attitude may sound "Tomish." It is fashionable for leftists to put down the American Dream. I was almost booed off the stage at Howard University in 1979 because of that comment. Yet most of the critics were expatriate Africans who were jeering because they didn't have the right to jeer anybody important at home. "You got yours; it's all right for you to say that," they said angrily. But the evidence is that the percentage of black youth unemployment hasn't moved (except up) since the Vietnam War closed down.

Sam Hill, a black penologist at San Quentin Prison, is a friend of mine. During one of my visits there, a black convict told me, "Some of those jive-ass black civil rights leaders don't know they ass from second base. When you ain't got no skill, ain't nobody gonna pay you $2.50 an hour [the minimum wage then]. That's why the brothers are here. The same with the [Mexican] Mafia. Them wetbacks come across the [Rio] Grande and break they backs in Del Monte's fields. But it ain't worth $2.50." He said that as a point of fact. Sam agreed.

We have become too psychologically dependent on the U.S. government and a few famous civil rights leaders, like Jesse Jackson, to solve our problems. This dependence started in earnest during the FDR days, as a holdover of the promises from World War I. One of my uncles told me, "We all thought things would be different after World War I because we fought well, but things didn't turn out that way. I remember them riots in 1919. We were real scared in some places in those days."

Well, the fear is gone, but the battered psyche lives on,

passed down to my generation of war babies. My generation of students who sat-in and marched and protested came down too hard on our parents. We forgot what they went through, what little power they had. My generation never lived through a Depression.

For years, I sought out the thoughtful, the powerful, and the privileged. Like Sisyphus, I never quite reached the summit. Winning Wimbledon and being ranked No. 1 in the world were great honors, and I even got to meet Queen Elizabeth and Princess Margaret, but I also knew they were only part of what I was pursuing. I once dropped a note to Elliot Richardson when he was the U.S. ambassador to Britain, asking if he wanted to have lunch with a group of American tennis players on the middle Sunday during the 1975 Wimbledon. To my surprise, he said yes. It was fascinating. He brought along Bill Clements, who was then under secretary of defense and now is governor of Texas. They answered questions freely for about an hour and a half.

I also went out of my way to meet Robert Ardrey, the author. I had heard he lived in Rome, so during the 1973 Italian Open, I called him and introduced myself. To my surprise, he said, "Come on over," so I had dinner at his house. Just like that. We talked about his books, and his theories on evolution. His books were fascinating, so I figured he would be also. And he was, no question about it.

World travel can reinforce prejudices, as it did for the British at the height of their empire. Or travel can also convince you, as Neil Armstrong learned from his celebrated walk on the moon, that all of us on Earth need each other and must share a common destiny. I believe that I was destined to do more than hit tennis balls. The abrupt end of my tennis career only accelerated my search for another way I can make a contribution. I don't want to be remembered mainly because I won Wimbledon.

There are a great number of people who don't like me, who feel I haven't done enough for certain causes or that I've chosen the wrong ones to support. I came along in the mid-sixties. I graduated from college in 1966 when at UCLA the white students were demonstrating their right to say "shit" and the black students in the South were sitting-in and marching for the right to sit at a lunch counter. Everybody was expected to pull his or her weight, and I wasn't very far out front as far as race or outspokenness were concerned in the mid-sixties. But I was geographically isolated at UCLA, bounded on the north by Bel Air, on the east by Beverly Hills, on the west by Santa Monica, and on the south by Westwood. There weren't too many blacks that live in that section of Los Angeles. Until I was a junior in college I never even had a car, so my life centered around life at UCLA.

I read about what was happening in Virginia because Virginia was my home state. But meanwhile, I was trying to be the best tennis player I could. All that changed when I made that political speech in Washington, as a lieutenant in the army. Once I got politically involved I wound up involved on an international basis because South Africa had denied me a visa to go to that country in 1969 and 1970. I became very engrossed in what South Africa was all about. People would say to me, "Why are you so concerned with something that is seven thousand miles away when we have problems right here at home?" My answer was that in this country, I can get involved in anything I want. Why do I have to concentrate on domestic black problems? Why can't I get involved in black problems internationally if I choose? If people really wanted to prioritize the various ethnic groups in the United States according to who needed help the most, they wouldn't even start with the American blacks. The American Indians are worse off than anybody. So when people got on me about South Africa, I would tell them, "Well, I never

215

see any of you guys out there protesting for the American Indian." I remember telling one guy, "It seems that Joan Baez and Marlon Brando do more than you do for the American Indian, who is beneath even us on the totem pole." He didn't have an answer. I said, "Look, I know the reason why you're not involved. Most of the Indians you see like the Apache or Cherokee or Sioux are on those crummy TV programs. Yet there is an Indian reservation in Virginia about thirty miles from where I lived."

What will the future hold for me? I will always stay involved with tennis and sports. It's what I do best and what I feel most comfortable with. I look forward to participating in the Davis Cup wars as captain. I know that I'm more of an idealist than any of my players, except possibly Stan Smith and Bob Lutz. But the task is to bridge the gap and try to bring the prestige of the competition back up to a higher level in the eyes of today's modern player.

I will always stay involved with junior tennis in some capacity. It may sound trite for an athlete to say this, but I do feel I have something to contribute. Even Dick Savitt, the former Wimbledon champion with whom I used to practice, would offer unsolicited advice. I listened because he was Dick Savitt, Wimbledon champion. He's now a stockbroker, but he still has a bit of the teacher in him.

I want to be my own boss; I want to sink or swim on my terms. Billy Talbert told me a story ages ago that I've never forgotten. "When I went to work for U.S. Banknote," Billy began, at a clambake at his mother-in-law's, "I asked to work on commissions only. That way, if I didn't work hard, I wouldn't make much money. It's like being thrown into the deep end of a pool if you can't swim. You either learn fast or you drown. Business requires the same attitude." Billy was right, of course. I once did some work for the Saxon Paper Company alongside Clark Graebner. Clark turned out to be a good salesman; I didn't, but I was working on a draw. When it didn't work out, I felt haunted by Billy's story. I won't make that mistake again.

I'll continue to write. I'm not sure what, but I enjoy writing. My *Washington Post* bi-weekly column has forced me to learn how to say concisely what I'm thinking. I feel fortunate to have a forum like the *Post* in which to air my views. There are several more books in me. I learned from John McPhee and Frank Deford that writing is an art. If you know how to do it and can do so with passion and conviction, you can write and write and write. I would never run out of subjects because my life and experiences are always changing. Of course, by the year 2000, books will begin to be anachronisms. Man's storehouses of knowledge will be encapsulated on discs and other more sophisticated means of information storage. You will be reading books on your TV screen instead of off your shelf. You'll be able to house as much knowledge on your memory storage devices as there are in high school libraries. Books will become works of art, not reservoirs of history. But somebody has to write these things, and I'll be around somewhere. I have always been in love with the English language and the power of the pen.

Elective political office used to intrigue me very much. But I've shied away from that now for a reason: the typical elective offices are not as influential as they used to be. Television, special-interest group support, and debt seem to tag along inextricably with officeholders. Candidates are now packaged rather than being allowed to be themselves. They take a poll, find out what the people are thinking, and then change their views to suit the results. Appearance counts more than substance. One hot issue can elect or defeat you, and I really don't have the temperament for all that now. I like me the way I am. I've got my vulnerabilities and foibles and character weaknesses. But I genuinely like myself. And besides, I'm now nomadic; to make a go of elective office, I'd have to stay put.

These are ups and downs in life, like the ebb and flow

of sets in a tennis match. When Ken Rosewall played his final match against Rod Laver in the 1968 Pacific Southwest championships, Rosewall won the first set 7–5, then never won another game in the match. The last two sets were 6–0, 6–0. Four years later, Rosewall beat Laver in the WCT final; this time the match went to five sets and Rosewall, who also beat Laver in the 1971 WCT final, won in a decisive tiebreaker, 4–6, 6–0, 6–4, 6–7, 7–6.

In that three-hour thirty-four-minute match, Rosewall was down in the tiebreaker 5–4, in the fifth set, with Laver serving. But Laver served twice to Rosewall's backhand, and "Muscles" won both points. He then served out the match. When you contrast the 1968 match with their 1972 final, you have two different kinds of matches, two different outcomes, and two different mental attitudes.

Perhaps the ultimate analogy between sports and life is illustrated in the way those two Laver-Rosewall matches were played. I seem to go through my existence in similar stages. And just as no one could have imagined that Rosewall in 1968 would not win another game, life also juxtaposes many completely unrelated experiences. I'm going to experiment with life for the next few years and then settle down again to some basics. Along the way, I hope not to lose sight of my time-honored values or shrink from personal responsibilities.

The peer pressure to become involved can be deadly. Many black athletes and entertainers who didn't do enough were criticized. Hank Aaron and Ernie Banks suffered unfairly at various stages of their baseball careers for not being more vocal. Not too many blacks were prepared to be thrust into the limelight that racial confrontation called for. You can actually do more harm than good if you say the wrong thing. But it was a very difficult time if you were black and were not overly militant. And then there were the South Africans who turned down my visas because I was too militant.

Then, Now, Hereafter

I have always tried to be true to myself, to pick those battles I felt were important. My ultimate responsibility is to myself. I could never be anything else. I hope that when people read my story they will at least understand how Arthur Ashe came to be who he is.

Arthur Ashe Open Tennis Career Highlights

COMPILED BY STEVE FLINK

1968

Tournaments Played	22
Tournaments Won	10
Record	72–10 .878
U.S. Ranking	No. 1
Season Highlights	U.S. Open Singles Champion
	U.S. National Singles Champion
	Member Victorious U.S. Davis Cup team, winning 11 of 12 singles matches.
	Semifinalist Wimbledon
	Finalist U.S. Open Doubles with Andres Gimeno

1969

Tournaments Played	26
Tournaments Won	2
Finals Reached	6
Record	83–24 .776
U.S. Ranking	No. 2
Season Highlights	Semifinalist Wimbledon
	Semifinalist U.S. Open
	Member Victorious U.S. Davis Cup team

1970

Tournaments Played	30
Tournaments Won	11

Finals Reached 3
Record 91–20 .820
U.S. Ranking No. 3
Season Highlights Australian Open Champion
Member Victorious U.S. Davis Cup team

1971

Tournaments Played 32
Tournaments Won 3
Finals Reached 6
Record 77–31 .713
U.S. Ranking No. 2
Season Highlights Semifinalist U.S. Open
Semifinalist Italian Open
Quarterfinalist French Open
French Open Doubles Champion with Marty Riessen
Finalist Wimbledon Doubles with Dennis Ralston

1972

Tournaments Played 31
Tournaments Won 3
Finals Reached 3
Record 69–30 .690
U.S. Ranking Not ranked (contract pros not ranked that year)
Season Highlights WCT Winter-Fall Playoff Champion
Finalist U.S. Open

1973

Tournaments Played 31
Tournaments Won 2
Finals Reached 7
Record 68–29 .701
U.S. Ranking No. 3
Season Highlights Finalist WCT Championship
Finalist ATP Championships
Finalist U.S. Pro Championships

Arthur Ashe: OFF THE COURT

1974

Tournaments Played	29
Tournaments Won	3
Finals Reached	6
Record	85–27 .759
U.S. Ranking	No. 5
Season Highlights	Stockholm Open Champion
	Bologna WCT Champion
	Barcelona WCT Champion
	Finalist U.S. Pro Indoor

1975

Tournaments Played	29
Tournaments Won	9
Finals Reached	5
Record	108–23 .824
U.S. Ranking	No. 1
World Ranking	No. 1
Season Highlights	Wimbledon Champion
	WCT Champion
	Semifinalist Grand Prix Masters
	Semifinalist U.S. Pro Championships

1976

Tournaments Played	28
Tournaments Won	5
Finals Reached	4
Record	64–23 .736
U.S. Ranking	No. 3
Season Highlights	Won 5 WCT Events

1977

Tournaments Played	5
Tournaments Won	0
Finals Reached	0
Record	6–5 .545
U.S. Ranking	Insufficient Data
Season Highlights	Australian Open Doubles Champion with Tony Roche

Career Highlights

1978

Tournaments Played	28
Tournaments Won	3
Finals Reached	1
Record	65–25 .722
U.S. Ranking	No. 9
Season Highlights	Finalist Grand Prix Masters
	Semifinalist Australian Open

1979

Tournaments Played	13
Tournaments Won	0
Finals Reached	2
Record	30–13 .698
U.S. Ranking	No. 5
Season Highlights	Finalist U.S. Pro Indoor
	Finalist U.S. Indoor

Summary

Tournaments Played	304
Tournaments Won	51
Finals Reached	42
Record	818–260 .751
Special Note:	Ashe was at least a finalist in 31 percent of the Open tournaments he played.

Davis Cup Record

1963 d. Orlando Bracamonte (Venez) 6–1 6–1 6–0

1965 d. Keith Carpenter (Can) 6–3 6–3 6–1 and Harry Fauquier (Can) 6–4 6–0 6–4; d. Rafael Osuna (Mex) 6–2 6–3 9–7 and Antonio Palafox (Mex) 6–1 6–4 6–4

1966 d. Lance Lumsden (British West Indies) 6–0 6–1 6–2 and Richard Russell (BWI) 8–6 6–4 8–6

1967 d. Marcelo Lara (Mex) 7–5 6–2 7–5 and Osuna 8–6 6–3 6–2; lost to Miguel Olvera (Ecua) 4–6 6–4 6–4 6–2 and Pancho Guzman (Ecua) 0–6 6–4 7–5 0–6 6–3

1968 d. Lumsden 6–1 6–1 6–0 and Russell 6–3 6–2 6–4; d. Osuna 6–0 6–3 6–0 and Joaquin Loyo-Mayo 6–4 8–6 6–2; d. Guzman 6–3 6–3 6–2 and Olvera 6–1 6–3 6–0; d. Juan Gisbert (Spain) 6–2 6–4 6–2 and Manuel Santana (Sp) 11–13 7–5 6–3 13–15 6–4; d. Premjit Lall (India) 6–2 5–7 6–2 6–4 and Ramanathan Krishnan (India) 6–1 6–3 6–3; d. Ruffels (Australia) 6–8 7–5 6–3 6–3 and lost to Bill Bowrey 6–8 7–5 6–3 6–3

1969 d. Ilie Nastase (Rumania) 6–2 15–13 7–5 and Ion Tiriac (Rum) 6–3 8–6 3–6 4–0 ret

1970 d. Wilhelm Bungert (Germany) 6–2 10–8 6–2 and Christian Kuhnke (Ger) 6–8 10–12 9–7 11–9 6–4

1975 d. Russell 6–2 6–1 6–2

1977 d. Roberto Chavez (Mexico) 6–4 6–4 6–4; lost to Raul Ramirez (Mex) 6–3 6–4 6–4

1978 lost to Bjorn Borg (Sweden) 6–4 7–5 6–3; d. Kjell Johansson (Swed) 6–2 6–1 6–4

Davis Cup Summary

Singles Matches Played	32
Singles Matches Won	27
Winning Percentage	.844

Wimbledon Record

1963 d. Carlos Fernandes 3–6 4–6 6–4 6–4 6–1, John Hillebrand 5–7 7–5 11–9 3–6 6–3; lost third round to eventual champion Chuck McKinley 6–3 6–2 6–2

1964 d. Milan Holecek 3–6 6–4 10–8 6–4, Cliff Richey 3–6 4–6 6–3 6–2 6–2, Bill Bond 6–4 6–4 6–0; lost fourth round to eventual champion Roy Emerson 6–3 6–2 7–5

1965 d. Doug Kelso 3–6 6–2 6–3 6–3, Pierre Darmon 6–8 6–4 6–4 6–1, Bob Carmichael 7–5 6–3 8–6; lost fourth round to Rafael Osuna 8–6 6–4 6–4

1968 (seeded 13th): d. Eduardo Zuleta 6–1 6–2 6–3; Ismail El Shafei 6–1 6–2 9–7; Ove Bengtson 11–9 6–4 6–1; John Newcombe 6–4 6–4 4–6 1–6 6–3; Tom Okker 7–9 9–7 9–7 6–2; lost semifinal to Rod Laver, eventual champion, 7–5 6–2 6–4

1969 (seeded fifth): d. Marty Riessen 1–6 11–9 6–3 7–5; Terry Ryan 3–6 4–6 6–3 6–2 6–2; Graham Stilwell 6–2 1–6 6–2 13–15 12–10; Pancho Gonzales 7–5 4–6 6–3 6–3; Bob Lutz 6–4 6–2 4–6 7–5; lost semifinal to eventual champion Laver 2–6 6–2 9–7 6–0

1970 (seeded third): d. Stilwell 6–3 6–3 6–1; Nikki Pilic 6–1 11–13 6–4 6–3; El Shafei 6–3 6–1 2–6 6–0; lost fourth round to Andres Gimeno 7–5 7–5 6–2

1971 (seeded fifth): d. Erik Van Dillen 3–6 6–3 6–4 7–5; Patrick Proisy 6–4 6–4 6–4; lost third round to Riessen 6–1 9–8 8–9 6–4

1974 (seeded 8th): d. Hans Kary 6–4 6–2 6–4; Teimuraz Kakulia 6–1 6–4 6–3; lost third round to Roscoe Tanner 7–5 6–3 8–9 6–2

1975 (seeded 6th): d. Bob Hewitt 7–5 3–6 6–2 6–4; Jun Kamiwazumi 6–2 7–5 6–4; Brian Gottfried 6–2 6–3 6–1; Stilwell 6–2 5–7 6–4 6–2; Bjorn Borg 2–6 6–4 8–6 6–1; Tony Roche 5–7 6–4 7–5 8–9 6–4; Jimmy Connors 6–1 6–1 5–7 6–4 for the title

1976 (seeded 2nd): d. Ferdi Taygan 7–5 6–4 7–5; Allan Stone 7–5 8–9 9–7 7–5; Mark Edmondson 7–5 6–2 8–6; lost fourth round to Vitas Gerulaitis 4–6 8–9 6–4 6–3 6–4

225

1978 (unseeded): lost first round to Steve Docherty 8–9 9–8 6–3 5–7 7–5

1979 (seeded 7th): lost first round to Chris Kachel 6–4 7–6 6–3

Wimbledon Summary

Tournaments Played	12	
Tournaments Won	1 (1975)	
Record	35–11	.761

Arthur Ashe Record in U.S. National Championships and U.S. Open

Until the emergence of Open Tennis in 1968, when amateurs and professionals were at last allowed to compete against each other, the pros were not permitted to compete at the great, traditional tournaments like the U.S. National Championships at Forest Hills and Wimbledon. As an amateur, Arthur Ashe first entered his national championships in 1959 at age sixteen. He continued playing in the Nationals through 1969, when it was last held. By that time, there was no longer a need for a separate U.S. National Championships because all of the best amateurs and professionals were battling each other at the U.S. Open. What follows is a summary of Ashe's record in both the U.S. National Championships and the U.S. Open. Arthur holds the distinction of being the only player to capture both events in one year. He did so in 1968.

U.S. NATIONAL CHAMPIONSHIPS

1959 lost first round to Rod Laver 6–2 7–5 6–2

1960 d. Robert Bowditch 6–4 8–6 6–4; lost second round to Eduardo Zuleta 6–4 6–2 6–2

1961 d. John Karabasz 6–2 6–2 9–7; lost second round to François Godbout 6–3 7–5 7–5

1962 d. Edward Newman 6–4 6–4 6–2; lost second round to second seeded Roy Emerson 6–2 6–3 6–0

1963 d. Alphonso Ochoa 6–4 5–7 6–4 6–4, Norman Perry 3–6 7–5 6–2 6–3; lost third round to Riessen 6–3 8–6 2–6 8–6

Arthur Ashe: OFF THE COURT

1964 (seeded eighth): d. Tom Okker 6–4 6–4 6–4; Lenward Simpson 6–0 6–2 6–0; Riessen 4–6 6–3 8–6 2–6 6–4; lost fourth round to Tony Roche 6–4 4–6 4–6 6–3 6–4

1965 (seeded fifth): d. Gene Scott 6–3 6–4 9–7; Gary Rose 6–0 6–3 6–2; King Lambert 6–1 6–3 6–4; Tom Koch 12–10 13–11 10–8; Emerson (No. 1 seed)13–11 6–3 10–12 6–2; lost semifinal to Santana 2–6 6–4 6–2 6–4—the No. 4 seed

1966 (seeded fifth): d. Lamar Roemer 15–13 6–2 6–0; Ron Holmberg 8–6 5–7 6–3 6–4; lost third round to John Newcombe 6–2 6–3 6–4

1967 did not play

1968 (seeded first): d. Chris Bovett 0–6 6–1 6–3 6–3; Ron Goldman 8–6 6–3 6–2; Humphrey Hose 8–6 6–3 6–3; Allan Stone 3–6 9–7 7–5 6–3; Jim McManus 6–4 6–3 14–16 6–3; Bob Lutz 4–6 6–3 8–10 6–0 6–4 in the final

1969 (seeded first): d. A. Cornejo 6–1 6–1; Dick Dell 6–4 8–6; Butch Seewagen 6–2 6–4; Stone 3–6 6–3 6–8 8–6 6–4; lost quarterfinal to Lutz 6–4 4–6 10–8 6–8 6–4

U.S. OPEN RECORD

1968 (seeded fifth): d. Frank Parker 6–3 6–2 6–2; Paul Hutchins 6–3 6–4 6–1; Roy Emerson 6–4 9–7 6–2; Cliff Drysdale 8–10 6–3 9–7 6–4; Clark Graebner 4–6 8–6 7–5 6–2; Tom Okker 14–12 5–7 6–3 3–6 6–3 in the final

1969 (seeded fourth): d. Dick Stockton 6–2 6–2 7–5; Dick Crealy 6–4 6–3 4–6 6–3; Jim Osborne 5–7 6–4 6–4 6–2; Manuel Santana 7–5 6–1 6–8 6–4; Ken Rosewall 8–6 6–3 6–4; lost semifinal to top seeded and eventual champion Laver 8–6 6–3 14–12

1970 (seeded seventh): d. Roscoe Tanner 6–7 6–4 6–3 6–4; Roy Barth 6–4 6–2 6–3; Okker 6–4 6–7 6–2 6–3; lost quarterfinal to Newcombe 6–1 7–6 5–7 7–6

1971 (seeded third): d. Dick Knight 6–3 6–4 6–1; Steve Krulevitz 6–2 6–1 6–1; Mark Cox 7–5 6–2 6–2; John Alexander 6–4 6–7 6–4 6–3; Manuel Orantes 6–1 6–2 7–6; lost semifinal to Jan Kodes 7–6 3–6 4–6 6–3 6–4

1972 (seeded sixth): d. Haroon Rahim 6–3 6–3 4–6 7–6; Bob Maud 6–4 6–4 7–6; Ross Case 6–4 6–4 3–6 6–1; Bob Lutz 5–7 7–5 6–4

6–3; Stan Smith (the No. 1 seed) 7–6 6–4 7–5; Cliff Richey 6–1 6–4 7–6; lost final to Ilie Nastase 3–6 6–3 6–7 6–4 6–3

1973 (seeded third): d. Colin Dibley 7–6 6–7 7–5 6–2; Sherwood Stewart 6–4 6–2 6–2; lost third round to Bjorn Borg 6–7 6–4 6–4 6–4

1974 (seeded eighth): d. Trey Waltke 6–3 7–6 6–2; Vitas Gerulaitis 7–6 7–5 6–2; Geoff Masters 2–6 6–2 6–3 6–3; Guillermo Vilas 6–7 6–4 6–4 7–5; lost quarters to Newcombe 4–6 6–3 3–6 7–6 6–4

1975 (seeded fourth): d. Victor Amaya 6–3 7–6; Vijay Amritraj 6–3 6–1; Zeljko Franulovic 6–2 6–0; lost fourth round to Eddie Dibbs 6–3 6–2 6–3

1976 (seeded seventh): d. John James 7–6 6–3; lost second round to Jan Kodes 6–1 6–2

1977 did not play

1978 (seeded sixteenth): d. Ross Case 4–6 7–6 6–1; Jiri Granat 6–2 6–3; Terry Moor 6–3 6–4; lost fourth round to Ramirez 6–4 4–6 3–6 7–6 6–2

U.S. National Championships Summary

Tournaments Played	10
Tournaments Won	1 (1968)
Record	25–9 .735

U.S. Open Summary

Tournaments Played	10
Tournaments Won	1 (1968)
Finals Reached	1 (1972)
Record	38–9 .807

Open Tennis Career Head-to-Head Records with 10 Key Rivals

17–8 vs. Tom Okker
11–6 vs. Stan Smith
 6–5 vs. Ilie Nastase
14–2 vs. Roy Emerson

Arthur Ashe: OFF THE COURT

5–5 vs. Guillermo Vilas
8–9 vs. Bjorn Borg
4–10 vs. John Newcombe
6–14 vs. Ken Rosewall
3–19 vs. Rod Laver
1–6 vs. Jimmy Connors

Amateur Highlights

U.S. Clay Court Champion 1967
U.S. Intercollegiate Champion 1965
U.S. Hardcourt Champion 1963

Junior Highlights

National Interscholastic Singles 1961
U.S. National 18 Indoors 1960–61

ATA National Titles

Boys 12 Singles 1955
Boys 16 Singles 1957–58
Boys 18 Singles 1960
Men's Singles 1960–63